Managing Database

FOUR CRITICAL FACTORS

Michael M. Gorman

QED Information Sciences, Inc.
Wellesley, Massachusetts

To Edward

© 1984 QED® Information Sciences, Inc.
QED Plaza ● P.O. Box 181
Wellesley, MA 02181

Library of Congress Number: 83-83114
International Standard Book Number: 0-89435-103-6

Printed in the United States of America.

Contents

Table of Contents

Table of Contents

Table of Contents

LIST OF ILLUSTRATIONS

List of Illustrations

Preface

Database is certainly here. Although it was first considered a highly technical subject, now, because of advanced tools, the technical complications of database are well hidden, and its real face, that of a management challenge, cannot be avoided.

During the past ten or so years there have been a number of excellent books on specific aspects of database, aimed at either technicians or management. There has not been published, however, a book that treats the critical management and technical issues of database in a single volume. This book is more than comprehensive, it is also uniquely constructed to examine database from four parallel constructed viewpoints.

This book contains material on the technology of database, the staffing required to implement database, the critical phases of the database project, and finally, the database management system (DBMS), which is the most likely software tool for database implementation. Each of these areas (technology, staffing, project, and DBMS) is addressed through four standard database components, which are: logical database, physical database, interrogation, and system control.

The result of using this standard component outline is that each topic is easily cross referenced from one chapter to the next. For example, in the technology chapter there is a logical, physical, interrogation, and system control component. Later, the staffing chapter defines the staff necessary to support these four components. The project phase chapters describe how these components are implemented to bring about an operating database. Finally, the book contains a thorough review of the facilities required for a comprehensive DBMS, again described in terms of these four components.

The book also contains a chapter on the proper role of data administration, and includes a complete job description for the database administrator. The book also contains a chapter that describes the risks when database is attempted in the wrong setting or at the wrong time. Suggestions are provided on how to control these risks.

To aid you in understanding how various DBMSs implement these respective database components, I have included an appen-

Preface

dix that compares popular DBMSs with respect to the database components.

Every concept contained in this book has been tested in performance many times on many client database projects during the past fifteen years, and tested as a collective database project methodology on several projects during the past two years. Types of projects tackled to date have included marketing, manufacturing quality control, and commercial banking. Thus, it is with the confidence derived from everyday work that I can recommend this book to you as a practical guideline for implementing successful database projects.

Acknowledgments

I would like to acknowledge the help of those who made this book possible. First, of course, there is my family, all of whom showed great understanding during the final year that it took to finish the book.

I am indebted to Matt Flavin for adapting Peter Chen's entity relationship diagrams for use in logical database design and for setting down the major parts of the logical database design process contained in Chapter 6. I also wish to thank Andre Jezierski of ITT for countless conversations over the years about database and how it should be accomplished. Thanks are owed as well to Ranga Rangarajan of the Bank of America, who enabled me to see the need for formally describing the data integrity and the data transformation models in terms of two database states: at-rest, and in-motion.

I am grateful to Art Chisholm, Bill Borst, Dan Prall, Larry Watkins, Scott Steele, George Harding, and to the staff of the Information Resources Group of the Biomedical Products Department of the Dupont Corporation in Wilmington, Delaware for providing the environment for ironing out the rough place: of the database project methodology contained in Chapters 5 t(8. Other DuPont personnel who provided help along the way were Jim Wells and Eugene Lambert. John Roby of U.S. Defense Logistics Agency provided a helpful review of the steps in the database project methodology. Lee Bushnell and Janet Bollier and of the Bank of America contributed a very helpful critical review.

Then there are the thanks I owe Chuck and Glenn Tesler of PROSOFT, for creating the ALLWRITE word processor, to Ron Malo, also of PROSOFT, who always had good suggestions on ALLWRITE's effective use. Additional thanks are owed to Phil Manfield of Conucopia Software for ELECTRONIC WEBSTER. Thanks too, to Dennis Jimmink of Radio Shack, who made sure that I never ran short of what I needed for the book's production.

I am especially grateful to Leona Robbins and her staff at QED for their constructive editing and book formatting suggestions. Finally, I wish to express my appreciation to John

Acknowledgments

Sullivan of my staff, and my son Michael, who both spent many days entering changes and producing the next "final" copy of the book.

1 Rationale for Database

1.1 THE DATABASE IN BUSINESS

A database is an expression of organization, clarity, and precision. It may or may not be computerized. If it is, it may exist on a microcomputer, a minicomputer, or a large mainframe. Finally, a database may or may not be centralized. Notwithstanding the mode, the mechanism, or the form of database implementation and operation, the codification of and adherence to data semantics, which are the rules for meaning, validity, and usage, are prerequisite to a successful database.

When a database is on a computer, it represents the automation of the knowledge component of a business, which is manifest through the business's quality operation, planning and management. With a successful database, management of a business can research the past, organize the present, and plan for the future. This book is all about how to achieve such a database.

1.2 TRADITIONAL DATA PROCESSING

The traditional data processing environment in the business world is normally program-centered. Systems are created of programs that read and update data records, sort, and then print. Often there are hundreds of steps in these large systems of programs.

Fundamentally, these systems are created on the basis of report needs. The first thing asked by system designers is "What do you want out?" Once the output is finalized, input specifications are nailed down, and once that is done, the programs are written to transform input to output. The result is a business system that exhibits these characteristics:

o The system collects only the data necessary for reports.

o It stores data only in prereport formats.

o It extracts data from its natural environment and stores it in formats efficient for the data processing required for reports.

o It represents all data semantics--rules for meaning, validity, and usage--through program logic.

o Its data files and programs are definitely interdependent as each is merely an extension of the other.

Whenever someone wants to change something major, everyone goes into a tailspin because:

o All the file formats have to change.

o A majority of the report programs have to change.

o A majority of the input programs have to change.

o A majority of the translation programs have to change.

In short, the entire system has to change. And since often there is not enough time, the programmer comes to the rescue and creates crafty solutions.

For example, if an age and handicapped status must be added to a personnel file, the sex code might be modified to conform to the one depicted in Figure 1.1. The programmer saves the day. In one swoop, all the programs that do not use the one-digit sex code do not have to be modified. And the programs that need the extra information from the sex code can be programmed to dig it out. The only programs that have to be modified are those that need male or female only. And in the cases of 1 to 8, the odd numbers are male and the even numbers are female. In the case of 9 and 0, programming work must be done. Finally, when the element is blank, it means that the person is under 5, either sex, and is not handicapped. All in all, were the database approach not available, this might be viewed as a good solution that avoids great amounts of reprogramming.

CODE	AGE			SEX		HANDICAPPED STATUS	
	0-5	6-25	26 & UP	MALE	FEMALE	YES	NO
1		X		X			X
2		X			X		X
3		X		X		X	
4		X			X	X	
5			X	X			X
6			X		X		X
7			X	X		X	
8			X		X	X	
9	X			X	X	X	
0	X			X	X		X

Figure 1.1   Crafty Sex Codes

Now for the bad news. Suppose the programmer does not complete the documentation of this crafty sex code before leaving the company. Further, suppose the age brackets must be changed to accommodate a new reporting requirement, and the handicap classifications must change to provide further differentiation. Of course, an update program must be created to change the sex code of all employees on their 26th birthday, and now personnel must code newborns of either sex 0 or 9, rather than 1 for male and 2 for female. Since the sex of those under five years old cannot be determined on computer printout, their sex has to be collected again when they become six.

What was originally intended to be a cost-effective solution to the problem of having to change all the programs becomes a real nightmare. There are two major problems with the crafty programmer solution:

o   A single data element has been made to perform three different jobs.

o   The rationale for assigning data values has been stored in only a few programs.

The first problem could be solved if there were a mechanism for changing the file without affecting the programs that do not actually use the changed data. The file could be changed to include the two additional data elements, handicapped status and age, without disturbing the sex element.

The second problem is much more serious. A standard access data file cannot be defined to contain the capabilities to reject or fix incorrect data usage for all programs that access it. Each program that accesses the file must have its own semantics, and that is precisely the problem. Once a data file has been updated incorrectly--and unknowingly--by personnel who have used a program that does not have the exactly correct, completely up-to-date semantics, the data file's overall integrity is flawed.

Whenever the environment of control and use of data spreads beyond a few individuals, the traditional environment of program-defined and program-enforced semantics is not viable.

1.3   OWNERSHIP ABSTRACTION

The example just cited would be simple to control and maintain if there were only one owner, one designer, one implementor, one user, and one maintainer, and if all these were the same person. Realistically, though, there cannot be a one-to-one relationship between computer systems and people. People not at all connected with the capture, storage, or maintenance of data want direct access.

The traditional method of file access is through a compiler language such as COBOL. Compiler languages are very expensive languages to use. A COBOL program of 50 pages is not uncommon. With 60 lines per page, at a cost of $40 per line, the average COBOL program costs $120,000. It is not hard to see why the search is on for both program and programmer replacements.

Direct access is now often accomplished through high-level, English-like noncompiler languages, sometimes called "natural languages." Although there are several different types, each requiring different amounts of human and machine resources, all natural languages share a common characteristic: greatly reduced creation and maintenance effort.

Some natural languages are easier to use than others. The easier ones, usually do not have extensive capabilities for branching, looping, terminal prompting, and the like. These simple natural languages are employed by managers and researchers rather than computer programmers. Other natural languages are more difficult to learn because they have extensive logic and selection capabilities, formatting, table look-ups, and other features. These comprehensive languages are more likely to be used by technical personnel or computer programmers.

With this multitude of languages, all capable of accessing the same database, there must be a single set of coherent policies to govern the definition and maintenance of the data. These policies need to exist right from the start, or more chaos will certainly result than there is now. And what we have now is quite enough.

The data therefore must be owned by an organizational level higher than all its users. And at that level, there must be a formally defined set of rules or policies for data definition, capture, and maintenance. The data must also reside within its natural contexts; it must not be pulled from these contexts as it is with traditional systems. Finally, each piece of data must say the same thing to all who utilize it. Figure 1.2 illustrates the effects on database applications when semantics and data are centralized or decentralized.

1.4 TRADITIONAL APPROACH PROBLEMS

The traditional approach to data processing system development has as its cornerstone the program, whereas the database approach to system development has as its cornerstone the database. Figure 1.3 depicts this difference. It is very important that the difference be clearly understood.

The Program as the Cornerstone

In the traditional approach, everything is owned by the programmer or the project. Under this ownership are the file, the input, and the output. Figure 1.4 illustrates the relationships of these system attributes.

The file, in the traditional system, is the data storage extension of the program. It is organized to help the program operate efficiently.

5

	Semantic control			
	Centralized		Decentralized	
	Data storage control			
Questions regarding distribution effects	Central-ized	Decen-tralized	Central-ized	Decen-tralized
Can data be shared among sites?	yes	yes	no	no
Is concurrent processing of the same data possible?	yes	no	no	no
Are common or corporate reports possible?	yes	yes	no	no
Can there be an overbear-ing "big brother" feeling?	yes	yes	no	no
Is there local control and ownership?	no	maybe	yes	yes
Do there need to be common data standards and policies?	yes	yes	no	no
Can local data require-ments be satisfied?	maybe	yes	maybe	yes

Figure 1.2   The Effects of Centralization and Decentralization
of Semantics and Data

The input to the traditional system collects only the data necessary to serve the output needs of the program. Often a one-to-one relationship exists between data collection and report generation. The data description of the file must be replicated in each data collection program.

The output is the inverse of the input. It too is produced by a program that contains a complete data description of the file upon which the report is based.

The program for the definition of the data consists of the file's description and whatever procedure division code is neces-sary to access the file and then to transform its contents for some output requirements. Finally, the data element, which is subservient to the file, which in turn is subservient to the program, has all its semantics defined in terms of the needs of the program.

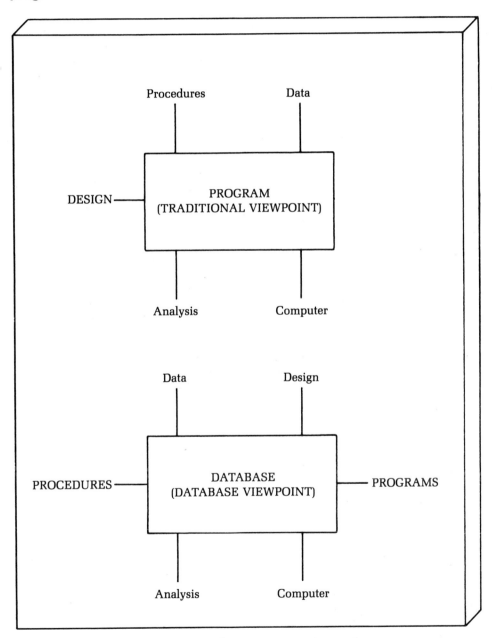

Figure 1.3 The Focus Has Changed

CHARACTERISTIC	APPROACH COMPARISON	
	Traditional data processing	Database approach
OWNERSHIP	Programmer	Corporation
FILE	Stand-alone, transient storage; & high-performance structure design	Permanent storage; small part of a naturally organized structure
INPUT	Only critical data to serve report needs; one data collection per report	Capture data and contexts; preserve environment and history; one data collection per database
OUTPUT	Multiple reports via single pass of data file	Transient report requirements that change often
PROGRAM	File division and procedure division with program-based semantics to process multimeaning data fields	COBOL only for updates and complex reports; ad hoc language; All semantics within the database
DATA FIELD	Small as possible; pack as many values & meanings as possible	Single meaning; well-defined with strict rules

Figure 1.4   Comparison of Attributes in the Traditional and the Database Approaches

The Database as the Cornerstone

The database approach has essentially the same components as the traditional approach, but defines and organizes each differently.

The database is an extension of the organization, rather than an extension of a program. It is permanent storage, and each of its record types has a meaningful life of its own. Each record type exists as a realized manifestation of an important policy. The structure of the database as a whole reflects that of the enterprise. To be permanent and useful, there should be a direct correlation between the quality of the database organization and the organization of the enterprise. In fact, the organization of the database cannot be better than that of the enterprise it models, since it merely reflects it.

The input to a database is always in the form of natural business transactions. Whole transactions are always included, never partial ones. The output from the database is unimportant. Each is a transient need expressed by some component of the enterprise to serve a temporal use. The programs that access the database should always be written in the most human-efficient language possible. When the integrity of the database is at stake, a language such as COBOL, which offers capabilities for complex processing, should be employed. Otherwise, any language will do. Finally, the data element, while subservient to the record type, serves only one mission, and it has the same meaning for all who use it.

Hierarchically, then, the database contains a single set of logically coherent data about a well-defined subject. Record types represent well-known, orthogonal, and rigorous policies within the context of the database. Fields represent well-known, orthogonal, and rigorous policies within the context of the record type. Figure 1.4 summarizes these points.

1.5 THE PROMISE OF DATABASE SYSTEMS

The database approach, when fully developed, offers these major organizational and technological benefits:

o Database systems, founded on organizational analysis rather than on process analysis, reflect organizational quality.

o Database designs preserve the natural contexts of business events.

o Databases last a long time: changes are minimal and have almost no impact on the programs that use data.

o Database systems offer a wide selection of "canned" software tools for manipulation of data. Each tool is designed to minimize human effort and to maximize overall database integrity.

9

o Database systems force the ownership of data to be escalated from the programmer to the organization.

o Database systems permit common, multiple-user data processing, with the database management system (DBMS) protecting the database from conflicting operations.

1.6 MEASURING DATABASE SUCCESS

The database approach can be viewed as either a management science or a technology. If it is understood only as a technology, it can certainly be implemented at any time, but its success can be characterized only by technological feats such as loading 5 billion characters, running 17 transactions per wall clock second, having 7 levels of hierarchy without any redundancy, or having only 1 record type represent 8 different purposes. These are measures of data processing success.

If, however, the database approach is understood to be a highly structured management discipline that employs computers as a major component of its implementation, then a successful database is characterized by organizational quality, coherent policy, efficient decision making, multipurpose high-integrity data, and by the multitude of ways in which functional users can collect present data, compare it to the past, and project future corporate strategies. These are measures of database success.

1.7 WHEN NOT TO USE THE DATABASE APPROACH

Database systems are well suited to all those data processing applications that are data-oriented rather than process-oriented. A data-oriented application is one that regards data as valuable in terms of its capture, manipulation, storage, and retention. In contrast, a process-oriented application uses data only for the purpose of controlling a process. Once the process is changed, the data has no residual value, so it is thrown away.

A data-oriented application also has no absolutely preordained, inviolate use for the data. The data may be useful for some other purpose later. To weld the data to a specific use, therefore, is not appropriate. In contrast, a process-oriented application has an absolutely preordained inviolate use for the data. The data may not be used for any other purpose later. It is therefore appropriate to weld the data to that specific use.

A data-oriented application is thus like a public library, whereas a process-oriented application is like a manufacturing plant. You cannot successfully use a process-oriented design technique to build a database, and you cannot successfully use a database-oriented technique to build process-oriented systems.

1.8 ORGANIZATION OF THE BOOK

The database approach, as an applied computer-based management science, consists of four components: the logical database, the physical database, interrogation, and system control.

The logical database component represents the logical organization of the database and the activities required to specify, implement, and maintain it. The physical database component represents the physical structure of the database and the activities that bring it into existence and maintain it. The interrogation component represents the various database management system (DBMS) data access languages and the activities required to choose the appropriate one for a task. Finally, the system control component represents the types of protections necessary to implement and maintain a database application.

Each of these four parts is presented in this book from four viewpoints: technology, staffing, project phases, and finally the DBMSs that carry out the computerization of database.

Chapter 2, on the technology viewpoint, defines what database terms mean. Chapter 3, on the staffing viewpoint, describes the staff that is needed for database component implementation. Chapters 5 through 8, on the project viewpoint, define the specification, implementation, and operation aspects of the database components. Chapter 9, on the DBMS viewpoint, defines how database components are implemented in a DBMS. In support of these views, Chapter 4 discusses the role database plays in the organization as a whole. Chapter 10 presents guidelines for controlling database risk. Finally, Chapter 11 summarizes the book and presents conclusions.

The interrelationships among the four database components, that is logical, physical, interrogation, and system control, and the four viewpoints, that is technology, staffing, project, and DBMS are presented in Figure 1.5.

VIEWPOINT	DATABASE COMPONENT			
	Logical	Physical	Interro-gation	System Control
TECHNOLOGY	Data model	Database creation & maintenance	Data selection & reporting	Audit trails, protection & evolution, etc.
STAFFING	Database specialist	DBMS specialist	Inter-rogation specialist	System control specialist
PROJECT	Conceptual specification phase Implementation phase Production and administration phase			
DBMS	Schema & sub-schema	Access methods, data loading, update, & maintenance	Query, host language, report writers	Utilities languages & techniques

Figure 1.5   Interrelationships among Four Database Viewpoints

1.9 REVIEW QUESTIONS

1. Summarize the problems with the traditional data processing environment.

2. Define ownership abstraction and explain, using examples, why such a definition might apply differently to different organizational units in a large corporation.

3. What are the advantages of direct data access using noncompiler languages such as query languages as opposed to indirect data access through host language interfaces such as COBOL?

Review Questions

4. What is the traditional method of file access?   Taking into account the likelihood of future changes in the system, is it possible to justify the costs of this form of file access?

5. Which fundamental components are similar in the traditional data processing system and the database approach? Which are different? Provide examples showing they are similar and different.

6. Describe how each of the six database advantages can benefit your organization.

7. Explain what is meant by the following statement: The quality of the database organization cannot be better than that of the enterprise that it models.

8. For what type of applications is the database approach best suited? Why?

9. In assessing the success of a database project, what major areas must be considered? Why?

10. In what instances would a database not be the logical or most economical solution to a data processing problem?

11. Using the example in this chapter or one from a typical work environment, state what is wrong with a programmer using tricks and crafty solutions to solve problems that emerge in large projects using many files and programs.

12. Why is the traditional approach to data processing wrong for database projects? Give examples.

2 Technical Viewpoint

2.1 DATABASE COMPONENTS

A database is most often implemented through a generalized computer software package called a database management system (DBMS). This chapter presents the technological concepts that are the basis of database and DBMS. The concepts presented here are also prerequisite to understanding the database project and its staffing requirements. Chapter 9 presents the technology of the database approach as viewed from the perspective of the DBMS, using a features-oriented approach.

The technical aspects of the database approach (and DBMSs) will be presented in relation to the four major database components: logical database, physical database, interrogation, and system control. Figure 2.1 presents these four components and their subcomponents. Figure 2.2 classifies the more popular commercially available DBMSs by database approach and data model.

2.2 THE LOGICAL DATABASE

The logical database is an expression of the data organization that is to be represented in the database. The logical data organization is expressed through record type structures and relationships that bind record structures together. The relationships are of two opposing types: static and dynamic. The complete data organization for a database is linguistically commu-

15

nicated to the DBMS through a data definition language. While each DBMS, upon detailed examination, has a unique logical data organization, these organizations can be perceived as belonging to one of four main data models. Two of the data models are static and two are dynamic.

DATABASE COMPONENT			
LOGICAL DATABASE	PHYSICAL DATABASE	INTERRO- ATION	SYSTEM CONTROL
Data Model	Storage structure	Host language interface	Audit trails
Data definition language	Access strategy	Procedure- oriented language	Message pro- cessing
	Data loading		Backup and recovery
	Data update	Query-update language	Security and privacy
	Database maintenance	Report writer	Reorganization
			Multiple- database processing
			Concurrent operations
			Installation and maintenance
			Application optimization

Figure 2.1   Database Management System Components

Record Structures

A data organization consists of a collection of element defini- tions called a record definition. When a record's elements are all defined to be single-valued, the record definition is said to

16

be simple. If some of the record's element definitions are to represent multiple values, such as "nicknames," or to represent a matrix such as "sales by month by year" for a particular product, then the record definition is said to be complex.

Data Model		Interrecord Relationship Mechanism			
		STATIC		DYNAMIC	
	Network	Hier-archy	Independent Logical File	Relational
Typical Systems	TOTAL IDMS (1) IDS DMS-2 DMS-1100 NCR-DMS	System 2000 IMS	INQUIRE ADABAS GIM FAMILY NOMAD FOCUS RAMIS MANAGE DMS-170 DATACOM	SQL/DS INGRESS ORACLE IDMS (1)

(1) IDMS has released its newest version (6.0) and it contains both traditional static network facilities and dynamic relational facilities. The relational facilities operate against its own relational structures and also against the network structures.

Figure 2.2   Classification of DBMSs

Relationship Types

Record occurrences themselves are also structured through inter-record relationships. For example, when the structure represents a COMPANY "owning" its PRODUCTs (see Figure 2.3), the defined relationship is hierarchical. When the defined record structure is such that a record is "owned" by multiple records, as in the case of the ORDER ITEMs being owned by PRODUCT SPECIFICATIONs, PRODUCT PRICEs, and ORDERs (see Figure 2.3), then the ORDER ITEM record is in a network relationship with its three owners. Finally, records may also be defined to be related to each other as "members," as in the case of all the

ORDER ITEMs that comprise the complete set of items on an order.

Relationship Mechanisms

The computer mechanisms that physically relate records in a network, a hierarchy, or as members are of two types. If the mechanism is based solely on element values, as in the case of a CONTRACT ID stored in each occurrence of the ORDER record, then its mechanism of relationship with the ORDERs record is said to be "value-based," and in this book is represented by a dashed line (see Figure 2.4).

Value-Based Relationships. The value-based relationship exists between two record types whenever the element upon which the relationship is based contains values that are acceptable to the rules stated in the relationship.

For example, the ORDER record with the element ORDER CONTRACT ID is related to the CONTRACT record with the element CONTRACT ID. A relationship exists between instances of these two record types if a CONTRACT record's CONTRACT ID element contains a value that is the same as the ORDER record's ORDER CONTRACT ID element. In this example, the relationship is one-to-many.

If a TEACHER's record contains a multivalued element TEACHER STUDENT ID and if the element contains a list of student numbers, then the relationship between a teacher and the related students is one-to-many. Similarly, if in the STUDENT record there is a multivalued element STUDENT TEACHER ID, then the relationship between an instance of a student and the related teachers is also one-to-many.

In a database system, if two records are related to each other in two one-to-many relationships, and if the semantics of the relationship are the same, then the relationship between the two record types is commonly named and is termed many-to-many. If however, the semantics of the two relationships are different, then the two relationships would remain both separately named and separately defined statements that represent record type interaction.

If the relationship is other than value-based, that is, if it is not represented by common data values, then the relationship is said to be "information-bearing." In this book information-bearing relationships are represented by solid lines (see Figures 2.3 and 2.4).

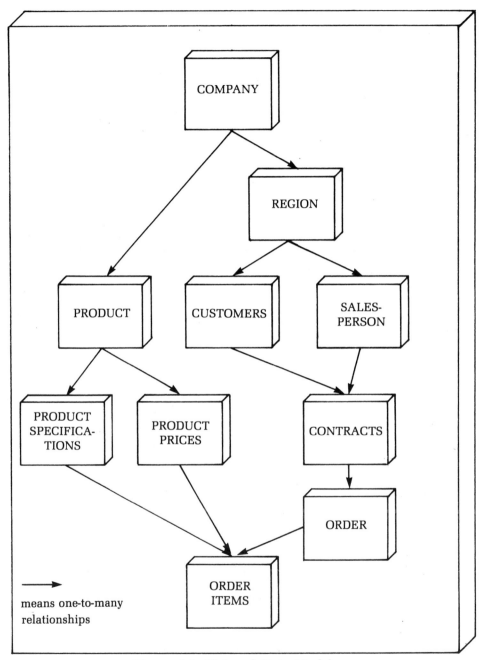

Figure 2.3   Network Data Model:
One Database with Nine Record Types

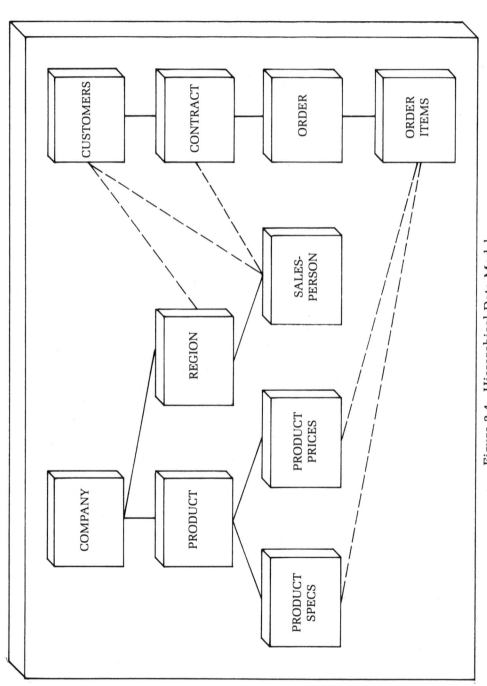

Figure 2.4   Hierarchical Data Model:
Two Databases with Six and Four Record Types Respectively

The Logical Database

Information-Bearing Relationships. Information-bearing relationships are so named because the relationships themselves convey information that normally cannot be verified through data values. For example, when the first ORDER record is retrieved for a given CONTRACT, it might be inferred that the first ORDER record represents the first ORDER placed under the contract, the second record represents the second ORDER, and so forth. In essence, the sequence of the accessed records represents information with respect to "when" the ORDER was placed.

The information-bearing relationship mechanism is normally controlled by the software system that performs the insertion and retrieval of records. In the case of a DBMS, the information-bearing relationship is normally a record's address within the file relative to the beginning of the file. This address is stored in the record's owner or prior member's record. This location is commonly referred to as a record's "relative record address."

As an example, if a record type's length is 100 bytes, and if each record is stored in a DBMS physical record that is 1000 bytes, there would be 10 logical records per physical record. If the relative record address of a record is 37, the record would be the seventh record of the fourth physical record. The relative record addresses of a record are stored during data loading or data update.

If a mistake is made regarding the order of the database records for ORDERs, a process that causes a physical reversal of the pointers that logically represent the order of the two records must be employed. For example, if the third ORDER is really the second, the second ORDER must be retrieved from the database into a computer program, its database representation deleted through a DBMS delete record command, and then the computer program's representation of the record stored back into the database "after" the next ORDER.

This physical control is in marked contrast to the user's control over the "value-based" relationship. For a value-based relationship, the simple process of changing the element's value also changes the relationship. For example, changing the value CONTRACT ID in an ORDER record occurrence automatically means that the ORDER instance belongs to another CONTRACT. If the chronological order is to be represented in a value-based relationship DBMS, the element ORDER DATE must be present so that when records are retrieved they can be sorted into chronological order by ORDER DATE.

Data Models

The organization of a database is represented by a language called the data definition language (DDL). This same language communicates the database's organization to the DBMS.

Since every DBMS's logical database is controlled by a certain set of rules, the totality of the rules that allow network or hierarchical relationships and that bind records through either value-based or information-bearing relationships is called the DBMS's data model.

In general, there are only four major data models. The network data model often is able to define complex records and allows a member record to be owned by multiple records (see Figure 2.3). The hierarchical data model generally defines only simple records and allows a member to be owned by only one owner (see Figure 2.4). For both data models, the relationships that bind records together are information-bearing.

The third data model, the independent logical file, stores complex records, but its mechanism of interrecord relationships is value-based (see Figure 2.5). The fourth data model, relational, stores only simple records and relates them through value-based relationships (see Figure 2.6).

Static and Dynamic DBMSs

The main reason for distinguishing between information-bearing and value-based relationships is that DBMSs, which are the predominant computer software tool for implementing databases, are grouped into two major categories: those that are essentially founded on information-bearing relationships, and those that are founded on value-based relationships.

Information-bearing relationship DBMSs create databases that are rigorously structured and that allow records to be retrieved and updated only in terms of these relationships. These information-bearing relationship DBMSs create a static environment, since the locations of the related records are already known.

The value-based relationship DBMSs create databases that allow the specification of relationships at retrieval time. The DBMS decodes the relationship specification and then proceeds to "discover" whether records exist that participate in this user-specified relationship. These value-based relationship DBMSs create a dynamic environment, as the locations of the related records are to be discovered during retrieval.

The Logical Database

Since both the network and hierarchical data models are based on information-bearing relationships that create static environments, these two models are generically referred to as static. Further, the DBMSs that represent these data models are called static DBMSs. Throughout the remainder of this book information-bearing relationships will be called static relationships.

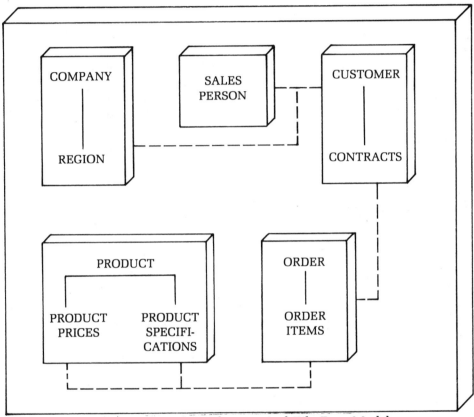

Figure 2.5 Independent Logical File Data Model:
Five Databases with Complex and Simple Record Types

Since the independent logical file and the relational data models are based on value-based relationships that create dynamic environments, these two models are generically referred to as dynamic. The DBMSs that represent these data models are called dynamic DBMSs. Throughout the remainder of this book, value-based relationships will be called dynamic relationships.

Technical Viewpoint

Static and Dynamic Data Models

As stated above, a data model is a formalized approach to the organization of data. As a result of allowed data structures, a data model allows only certain types of operations against the structures. Since a complete presentation of database operations by a data model would unduly lengthen this section, only the four basic data structures are presented. This has the unfortunate aspect of indicating that, for example, IBM's Information Management System (IMS) and INTEL's SYSTEM 2000 are exactly the same kind of data model, which is not true. They are equivalent generally, but not exactly.

A study of data models is important. Each model permits a certain number of information-bearing relationships between record types. Beyond these, the database designer's only option is to create value-based relationships that are under the control of the resultant application code/programs.

The number and variety of static (information-bearing) relationships are greatest in the network data model and least (none) in the relational data model.

Static Relationships. A static relationship (heretofore called information-bearing) is one that is declared explicitly by the database designer--through the DDL--and is then automatically generated by the DBMS whenever the owner is created and one or more members of the relationship are inserted. The relationship is usually a relative record address. Traditionally, this address is stored in the owner for its first member. Then the address of the "next" member is placed in the prior member. If a backward pointer is desired, the address of the prior record is stored in the next member. Finally, if the owner's address is desired, it is stored in each of the member records. If the relationship is a ring, then the final next pointer points to the owner. These DBMS generated pointer relationships are built as the records are loaded into the database, and are maintained through the process of update.

One advantage of a static relationship is the speed with which the DBMS can locate and retrieve the members of a relationship whenever a relationship traversal is invoked by a DBMS operation.

A disadvantage is that whenever the record's relationship with an owner and its next and prior members needs to be changed, the record's owner, and its next and prior members must all be retrieved and have their pointers changed to reflect

24

the removal of the record. Then, the owner, next, and prior members of the record's new location must be retrieved and have their pointers changed to reflect the inclusion of the new record.

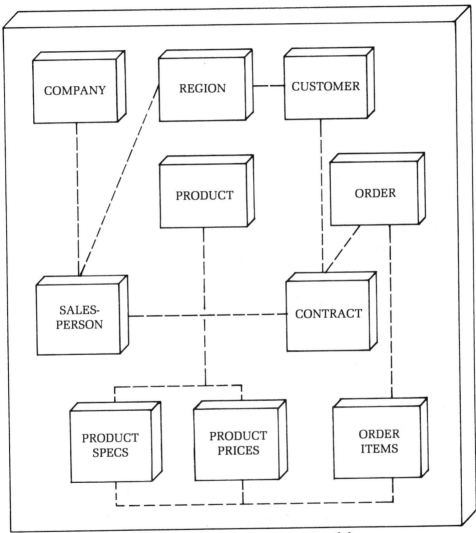

Figure 2.6   Relational Data Model:
Nine Simple-Record-Type Databases

Dynamic Relationships. In contrast to the static relationship, the dynamic relationship (heretofore called value-based) is one that is optionally declared by the database designer. It consists solely of an element value that exists in both the owner and the member record. Since the relationship consists of only an element value, the relationship may be changed through a simple update. While changing a relationship is very simple, more computer resources are generally required to traverse the dynamic relationship than required by the static relationship. This is because the dynamic DBMS must discover the location of the "related-to" record by finding out which record contains the value that is the basis of the relationship. In contrast, the static DBMS traverses the relationship much more quickly because the location of the "related-to" record is already known, since it is the "owner," "next," or "member" pointer that is stored in the "related-from" record.

Static Data Models. The network and hierarchical data models are founded mainly on static (information-bearing) relationships. Within a database the relationships are static. Between databases the relationships are dynamic. There are very few dynamic relationships within the network data model, simply because the database's relationship-modeling capability is naturally greater. An owner record type can have multiple member types, and a member type can be owned by multiple owner types.

Network. The network data model has several major versions. Notable among these is the Conference for Data System Languages (CODASYL) model, which has been implemented in slightly different variations by Honeywell (IDS-2), Univac (DMS-1100), and Cullinet (IDMS). The CODASYL data model has been the subject of intense study and evolution since 1969. The American National Standards Institute (ANSI) committee, X3H2, is working with a variant of this model and voted in June, 1984 that it should become an ANSI network data model standard. Other network data models are represented by CINCOM's TOTAL and the Burroughs DMS-2.

In general, the network data model allows multiple relationships between an owner and its members, among members of the same and different types with and without an owner, and between owners and members of the same type. Relationships that do not have another record type as an owner are called singular. Relationships that have the same record type as both owner and member are called recursive.

26

The Logical Database

Hierarchy. The hierarchical data model represented by IBM's IMS and INTEL's SYSTEM 2000 is simpler than the network data model because member record types in a hierarchy can have only one owner and there can be only one relationship between an owner and its members. Whenever a connection between hierarchical databases is required, a dynamic relationship must be created (see Figure 2.4). For example, the relationship between PRODUCT and PRODUCT SPECIFICATION record types is static, but the relationship between PRODUCT PRICE and ORDER ITEM record types is dynamic. The structure of the hierarchy record type is normally simple.

Dynamic Data Models. The independent logical file (ILF), illustrated in Figure 2.5, and the relational data models, illustrated in Figure 2.6, are based on dynamic relationships. The ILF data model typically can contain complex records. The relationships between record types are represented through shared data values. Figure 2.2 lists some of the popular ILF systems. A relational data model has only simple records and, like the ILF data model, represents interrecord relationships through data values.

ILF Data Model. An ILF database (typically a synonym for record type) is restricted to only one record type. Unlike the hierarchy, the ILF data model normally does allow a member record type to be complex. But the complexity is usually restricted to just two levels--a CUSTOMER and his CONTRACTs (see Figure 2.5), for example. The additional level of ORDERs for the CONTRACTS would normally not be allowed in the independent logical file data model. That could be accomplished only by adding another database and then connecting the first database to it through a dynamic relationship. For example, in Figure 2.5 the COMPANY database (record type) contains a repeating group, REGION. The relationship between the SALESPERSON and the REGION record types is dynamic. That is, the REGION ID from the REGION record is also present in the SALESPERSON record.

Some ILF DBMSs do allow record types more complex than two levels. However, because the effective use of these additional levels is severely restricted, and because their vendors strongly advise users not to use more than two levels, they are considered to be two-level systems.

Relational Data Model. The fourth data model, the relational, is the simplest. A relational database is restricted to a single, simple record type, called a relation. All relationships between record types (relations) must be dynamic. For example, in Figure 2.6, the SALESPERSON record type is related to the CONTRACT record type by the SALESPERSON-ID stored in the CONTRACT record type.

X3H2 is also working to standardize the relational data model. When it is standardized, possibly in late 1984, the two most important data models will be completed.

Dynamic Data Model Summary. Since each application of a dynamic DBMS contains no fixed relationships except within each of the dynamic databases, a database that consists of multiple dynamic databases could be dynamically configured to "appear" to have a data model that is a hierarchy to one user, a network to a second user, and another kind of network to a third.

Static and Dynamic Summary. Figure 2.2 presents the four data models, categorized as static or dynamic, and the major DBMSs associated with each data model. Figures 2.3 through 2.6 present examples of each of the four data models. The solid lines represent static DBMS-generated relationships. The dashed lines represent value-based relationships.

Static and Dynamic Applications

Static or dynamic relationships usually predominate a database application. Seldom is there an application in which the quantity of relationship types is evenly divided. That simply means that applications too are typically termed as either static or dynamic. Figure 2.7 tabulates the critical differences between static and dynamic applications.

If the application is static, then the relationships among record types are normally all well-defined, stable, and seldom-changing. Static applications also tend to be production-oriented, with large volumes and high velocities. The principal access languages for static applications are COBOL and FORTRAN.

A dynamic application, in contrast, tends to have relationships that change almost as often as the data. The orientation of the application is MIS (management information system). These applications often seem to have less data, lower volumes, and lower velocities than the static applications. Natural languages dominate the dynamic application.

	STATIC DATABASE	DYNAMIC DATABASE
APPLICATION	PRODUCTION	MIS
ORIENTATION	Centralized Corporate wide	Decentralized Department/Section/ Project
	Long development Long life span	Short development Short life span
DESIGN CHANGE	Seldom	Often

Figure 2.7 Comparison of Static and Dynamic Applications

A dynamic DBMS's DDL usually does not contain formally defined relationship clauses with all the attendant integrity, record storage, and retrieval subclauses. Record instances are stored in the record types in the order presented, and are maintained in any order, or they are stored and maintained in the order of the record's primary key. The user of a dynamic database has sort clauses as a fundamental part of the language. Records are thus selected and sorted before presentation. Once presented, the records should be able to be re-sorted and re-presented. Actually, the records are not sorted; their address pointers are.

The effect of having a dynamically related set of records is the inverse of the effect of having a statically related set of records. Each interrogation has an equal chance of retrieval and update efficiency. There is no bias to the processing. Often there are no restrictive relationship integrity clauses. That burden is placed on the user simply because it is the nature of the dynamic database to have the rules for record interrelationships undefined, and thus it must follow that the integrity clauses governing the interrelationships must also be undefined.

Knowledge of a DBMS's data model is important, but not as important as knowing whether the DBMS creates static or dynamic relationships. If the DBMS's relationships are static and the application is dynamic, application failure is almost always the outcome. If however, the DBMS's relationships are dynamic and the application is static, then the application usually is implemented, but the production rates normally fall far below expectations.

Data Definition Language

The data definition language (DDL) tends to be tailored to the DBMS's data model, whether its record types are simple or complex and whether its relationship mechanism is static or dynamic.

A static DBMS DDL is likely to contain a more comprehensive set of editing and validation clauses that affect multiple record types than is contained in a dynamic DBMS's DDL. In a dynamic DBMS the clauses relate only to a single record type. Some dynamic DBMSs allow for a central schema of multiple dynamically connected record types. In such a case, the dynamic DBMS DDL becomes more like its static DBMS counterpart.

In short, the quality and comprehensiveness of the data definition language inversely affects the number of programs that have to be written to accomplish data loading and then ongoing data update. An inverse relationship also exists between the robustness of the DDL and the amount of application program logic for editing, validation, integrity checks, and the like that must be included in each program or module.

Logical Database Summary

The logical database allows expression of the data organization that is to be in the database. The language that communicates this data organization to the DBMS is called the data definition language (DDL). Finally, the two different mechanisms of relationships that bind records within the organization are static (information-bearing) and dynamic (value-based). Within the static mechanism, the two data models are network and hierarchy; within the dynamic, the two data models are independent logical file and relational.

2.3 THE PHYSICAL DATABASE

The physical database, the second component of a database system, consists of five separate subcomponents. Each relates to the creation and maintenance of the physical aspect of the database. The preceding section, Logical Database, presents material relating to the logical (that is, the organization's) view of the database. The physical database material relates the DBMS's and the computer's view.

The Physical Database

Storage Structure

The storage structure of a database is the architecture of its physical construction. It consists of four parts: dictionary, indexes, relationships, and data.

The dictionary is the repository of the information represented by the compiled DDL. Many types of information are contained in the dictionary--validation rules and extra space lists, for example. Each DBMS's dictionary is unique. This component is created when the database's schema is created, and it is maintained automatically by the DBMS during various processes. Some DBMSs take the dictionaries for each database and store them in a "super" dictionary that is most often called a "data dictionary."

Indexes are mechanisms for fast access. They exist either as primary indexes (unique value guaranteed) or secondary indexes (repeated values allowed). Indexes usually point either to the relationships that exist as distinct and separate from the record types (of course, only static), or to the actual records (both static and dynamic). This component is automatically created during database loading, and is automatically maintained during update.

Relationships are the connections between record occurrences. If the relationship is static, then it is usually a relative record address that is stored in the owner (pointing to the member) or the member (pointing back to the owner or to the next member). If the relationship is dynamic, then the data value that is uniquely contained in the owner is replicated in many members.

Relationships are automatically created by the static DBMS, derived both from knowledge inferred from data record loading sequences and from special data loading verbs. In a dynamic DBMS, relationships among records exist implicitly as shared data values.

Subsequent to database loading, the static DBMS relationships are maintained through special user language verbs. In a dynamic DBMS, relationships are maintained through data element value changes.

The data part of the storage structure contains the occurrences of records. Generally, static DBMSs have multiple record-type data storage structures. In dynamic DBMSs, the general tendency is to have a separate data storage structure for each record type. This component is created and maintained as records are stored during load or update.

Technical Viewpoint

Knowledge of the storage structure is important because it indicates the power of the DBMS for certain applications. Some are well-suited for static applications, others for dynamic. If a static application is implemented with a dynamic DBMS, and if there are a large number of record types and a great volume of data, then the dynamic DBMS's storage structure that is most often designed for the simple, low volume application will probably not be able to handle a complex relationship and record ordering report efficiently.

Access Strategy

An access strategy is a collection of routines that insert data into and retrieve data from the database. The access strategy naturally falls into place once the storage structure is understood.

Understanding a DBMS's access strategy is the key to knowing why certain operations take longer than others, especially when they seem to be equivalent--and more importantly, when apparently similar operations produce different results.

Data Loading

Data loading is the process of inserting large quantities of data into the database at one time. DBMSs usually have special utilities to accomplish this task. Of special importance are the safeguards that may or may not be present when the data load utility is running, and the kinds and types of statistics that are produced once loading is accomplished.

Some DBMSs allow data to be loaded in certain ways to achieve efficiencies during subsequent updating and reporting. This is called load engineering.

Data Update

Every database requires updating. An understanding of how the storage structure reacts to certain types of updates is essential to the effective selection, design, and implementation of applications for a particular DBMS.

Critical to application performance is how well the DBMS handles additions of new records, deletions of existing records, modification of relationship occurrences (not types: that is reorganization), and modification of element values. It is important to know how the DBMS access strategy accomplishes each update type, so that the application can be designed in the most efficient manner. It is also important to note the efficiency with which auxiliary structures, such as indexes and relationships, are changed as the data are changed.

Database Maintenance

Database maintenance refers to the creation of a backup copy of a database. While creating a backup is certainly the first step in backup-and-recovery, a topic in system control, the nature of the backup process, needs to be understood so that sufficient resources can be allocated to its accomplishment.

The number of storage structure units that constitute individual databases varies widely. In general, when a DBMS is static, the number is small; in a dynamic DBMS, the number tends to be large. Because of this variation, and because one application may in fact require multiple physical databases to contain its logical database data, the backup process must be understood so that sufficient resources and time can be allocated and scheduled to adequately carry out the database backup process.

Physical Database Summary

The physical database is the component of database that confirms the computerized version of the logical database and represents the process of database loading, ongoing update, and database backup.

2.4 INTERROGATION

Interrogation is the third component of a database system. When DBMSs were first developed in the late 1960s, there were only two kinds: those that accessed data through self-contained or natural languages, and those that accessed data through host language interfaces (HLIs). A natural language in this sense is a special language invented by the DBMS vendor to replace a compiler host language, like COBOL, as the database access language. From about 1965 to 1971, there were DBMSs that had only one of these types of languages to both access and update data.

Today most DBMSs have a variety of access languages. Selection of the right language is important. A database programmer might choose a natural language because it takes only a fraction of the human effort required for the same program

33

coded in COBOL. Conversely, one might choose the COBOL interface language because its sophisticated processing and reporting capabilities are needed. Or COBOL might be chosen because the natural language is not at all DBMS-independent. Thus, when a natural language task is moved from one database environment to another, the task will very likely have to be recoded.

Determining the proper use of each DBMS language is important. For example, natural languages should be used for short-lived, simple tasks; compiler languages such as COBOL should be used for the long-life, complex tasks that require portability.

The static or dynamic nature of a database has a profound effect on language design. Generally, static systems utilize languages that report and process data according to the dictates of the database's structure, while dynamic systems allow users to express structure relationships and then report and process from the DBMS-found data.

2.5 SYSTEM CONTROL

System control is the fourth and last component of database. Its goal is to protect the DBMS, the database, and the application. These protections include audit trails, message processing, backup and recovery, reorganization, multiple database processing, concurrent operations, security and privacy, installation and maintenance, and application optimization.

Audit Trails

An audit trail is a time-ordered and user-sequenced record of reprocessable update operations that are executed against the database. Without an effective and complete audit trail, there may be no way to determine the source of a destructive update.

Message Processing

In a database application there are many sources of messages: the DBMS, the operating system (O/S), various pieces of system software, and the application itself. The sources of these messages must always be determined, and there should be a central scheme for their definition, maintenance, and issuance. This scheme should ideally be a database so that users can access a message to determine its meaning.

System Control

The messages are of three basic types. Informational messages usually inform the user that the command or operation is successful. Data and syntax errors indicate that the command or operation was rejected, and should be resubmitted. Database structure and DBMS program errors usually indicate that a major, unrecoverable error has occurred. In either case, the DBMS usually aborts its operation, and the database administrator must be summoned to determine the extent of the damage and to recover the situation.

Backup and Recovery

Database errors occur mainly during update. An update may not be successfully completed because there has been a computer hardware failure, or because of a bug in the system software, the DBMS, or the application. In addition to these types of failures, there may have been updates that are mistakes (for example, a whole group of customers may have been assigned to the wrong salesperson's territory). Under any of these situations the database may have to be moved "back" in time to a state in which the errors did not occur. Backup and recovery capabilities are usually a combination of manual and DBMS-based procedures performed by the database administrator.

The four types of database recovery are: reprocessing the complete programs that accomplished the updates against a database backup; processing a special constructed, centralized file of DBMS storage structure changes against a database backup (roll-forward); processing a file of "before" images to bring the database from a current state to a prior state (roll-back); and a combination of roll-back and then roll-forward.

The capabilities provided by the DBMS for backup and recovery of on-line and batch update tasks are critical to the establishment of a stable application environment. Naturally the users' central database administration group plays a critical role during database damage situations.

Reorganization

There are two types of reorganization: logical and physical. Both are required from time to time in any database environment. Logical database reorganization is the creation, deletion, or modification of element characteristics, record characteristics, or relationship characteristics. Logical database reorganization often causes physical reorganization.

35

Technical Viewpoint

When a database is initially loaded, all the storage structure components are in an optimum order. All index pages are in a physical order that mirrors the logical order, all data records are appropriately close to their owners, and so on. Over time, database updates cause the indexes, data records, and other storage structure components to be in a less-than-optimal order. This disorganization is usually not serious at first, but after a while an application can just stop performing its functions and operations quickly.

Most DBMSs have reorganization capabilities. Some are advanced enough to have different capabilities for each storage structure component. The benefit of this level of granularity is that a specific storage structure component can often be reorganized at low cost, providing a significant performance boost to the entire application.

Concurrent Operations

The essence of the database approach is concurrent operations-- that is, multiple DBMS functions operating on the same database at the same time with different languages and different operation modes.

Much of the functionality of concurrent operations is in the operating system software. Some operating systems allow the multiple access of a storage structure component directly--with protection--and others do not. As a result, DBMSs operating under different operating systems implement concurrent operations differently.

Concurrent operations can include operations on the logical database, the physical database, the various interrogation languages, and the various system control functions such as message processing, audit trails, and reorganization.

Multiple Database Processing

Multiple database processing is the ability to access data from different databases from within the same host language interface (HLI) or natural language run-unit. Multiple database processing is needed, for example, to interrelate data from different databases that may belong to different departments of the same organization, or to interrelate databases from different years.

Most dynamic DBMSs have very well-developed multiple database processing capabilities. This is because dynamic DBMSs require multiple database processing to accomplish any significant database applications. The dynamic DBMSs allow this multiple database processing through a variety of interrogation languages.

In static databases, however, the databases are naturally more complex, so their DBMSs usually provide this capability only through the host language interface--typically a language like COBOL or FORTRAN.

Security and Privacy

Database use necessitates sophisticated security and privacy. Database systems centralize diverse data, preprocess important relationships, provide indexes for fast access, and allow access through easy-to-use languages. Security, therefore, must be available in different types, levels, and methods; its establishment and maintenance must also be easy to learn and use.

Installation and Maintenance

Most installations have multiple versions of a DBMS, each suited to a particular application type. One version, for example, might be stripped of all update modules as an extra security measure. Another might be completely "flat" (no overlays) for a special kind of bulk update.

In addition to DBMS installation activities, this system control component also includes the categorization, analysis, and resolution of any DBMS bugs.

Application Optimization

Once the database application is implemented, certain functions are apt to run slower than others. Determining the exact cause of a slowed function is difficult because of the inherent interacting complexities of the DBMS, the database, and the application.

Some DBMSs have special sets of utilities to produce statistics about the performance of their own operations. Included would be input/output (I/O) counts, central processing unit (CPU) seconds, overlay swaps, and structure navigations. The purpose of these utilities is to learn how the DBMS reacts to a specific application configuration. This information can then be used to optimize the application code that processes the database, the design of the database, and the use of the DBMS. The more closely a database design is tuned to one of its applications, the more out of tune it tends to be with others, unfortunately.

System Control Summary

The system control component of a database system is clearly in a supporting role. Nonetheless, the role is absolutely critical to efficient and correct database application operation. None of the system control topics can be ignored without certain disaster at some time in the future.

2.6 TECHNICAL VIEWPOINT SUMMARY

A database management system is normally the vehicle for implementing a database system. That simply means that a database must exist as a complete specification before it can be computerized through a DBMS. A DBMS does not automatically provide a database environment, however; it merely facilitates it. An organization must engage in serious planning, analysis, and soul-searching before it can make effective use of a DBMS.

Although tremendous amounts of literature have been written on the subject of different data models, the data model of a DBMS is not nearly as important as knowing its fundamental method of relationship definition, creation, and maintenance--that is, whether it is static or dynamic.

The logical database component of the DBMS incorporates the organization's definition of the structure of the database and creates a computer-based dictionary that is then used by the other three DBMS components. The physical database component permits the actual database creation, loading, update, and backup. Interrogation includes all the languages that access the database. Finally, the system control component of the DBMS offers multiple safeguards and protections. As an integrated entity, the DBMS incorporates the computer tools necessary to implement the database project, once that project has been fully and correctly analyzed and designed.

2.7 REVIEW QUESTIONS

1. What are the four main components of a DBMS? Define each, and explain how they interact.

Review Questions

2. List the four general data models in order of complexity. Describe two examples of each type.

3. Define and compare static and dynamic relationships. Show the advantages and disadvantages of both.

4. What is the role of a DBMS's data definition language (DDL)?

5. Name and briefly summarize the importance of each component of the storage structure. What are the functions provided by each?

6. Why is a good understanding of access strategy important?

7. What is meant by data loading and data update?

8. Compare the advantages and disadvantages of using a natural language with those of using a host language interface.

9. What is the ultimate goal of system control?

10. When using a database with a faulty or inadequate audit trail, what are the risks?

11. What is the main function of backup?

12. What is the major benefit of a database application with good message processing?

13. Name and describe the two types of reorganization.

14. Describe the role and function of application optimization?

15. Briefly summarize the interaction between the four database components and the role a DBMS does and does not play.

3 Staffing Viewpoint

3.1 REQUIRED DATABASE PERSONNEL

Since a database project is different in important respects from a traditional data processing project, the staffing required to undertake it is also different. Five different types of skilled persons should be represented in a database administration (DBA) group.

A database specialist is needed to help functional users create a complete database design. An interrogation specialist is needed to assist in users selecting and then utilizing the most appropriate DBMS access language for loading, update, and retrieval. A system control specialist is needed to represent, design, and implement the proper protections, safeguards, and optimizations, and then to verify that they are present in each database application. A documentation and standards specialist is needed to ensure that applications are implemented in a consistent and uniform manner in order to enhance data and program interchange. Finally, a DBMS specialist is needed to install, test, configure, and fix the DBMS, and to ensure that applications are created that utilize the DBMS in the most efficient manner.

3.2 THE DATABASE SPECIALIST

A great deal of functional knowledge is required to design a correct and useful database. Therefore, the database specialist's expertise would be primarily in the functional area of the data-

41

base. For example, if the database were about contracts accounting and administration, the database specialist would be expected to be completely knowledgeable in that area.

The database specialist does not design the database; he or she consults with and assists the various functional users in designing it. The method by which the specialist guides them through the database design method is described in Chapter 6.

After the database is designed, the database specialist helps develop a complete implementation plan that is realistically founded on a complete conceptual specification. The conceptual specification consists of a complete database design (the logical database) and a preliminary analysis of the other three components--the physical database, interrogation, and system control.

During implementation, the database specialist finalizes any database design details that may not have been addressed during the conceptual design process. Each changed detail that affects policy must be cleared with the functional users.

An important step in the implementation plan is the transformation of the generalized database design to a specialized design required by the DBMS. The database derived during the conceptual specification stage is very often a network, so an analysis is required to determine whether the relationships that bind the network of record types together are mainly static or mainly dynamic before the appropriate DBMS that is to be used for database implementation can be chosen.

Regardless of whether the DBMS is static or dynamic, if the DBMS employed is a hierarchy, an ILF, or relational, additional policies regarding integrity must be developed to permit construction of the DBMS's version of the database. These additional constraints need to be formally documented as thoroughly as any of the other database policies.

The database specialist must oversee this transformation process and make absolutely sure that none of the policies established by functional area users are compromised.

3.3 THE INTERROGATION SPECIALIST

The role of the interrogation specialist seems almost traditional. This person can utilize any of the standard methods of design on database subsystems (the data loading, data update, and reporting subsystems).

Since the literature contains volumes regarding ways to design a subsystem, the subject need not be addressed here.

The most critical aspect of the design of either the data loading or the data update subsystems is that the policies utilized must first be designed during the conceptual specification phase of the database project.

If a policy flaw is discovered during the design or implementation of any aspect of the database project, be it an omission or a conflict, the interrogation specialist must not fix it. The flaw must be referred to the database specialist for resolution. If the interrogation specialist fixes the policy flaw, then the same situation that plagued the standard access application with three different uses of the sex code (described in Chapter 1) could surface again.

Once the loading and update subsystems have been constructed for a particular database project, the interrogation specialist assumes the role of a consultant to various users of the database as they develop and maintain reporting subsystems that come and go during the lifetime of the project. As a consultant, the interrogation specialist helps users select the most appropriate access language and assists them through design, coding, testing, and documentation.

3.4 THE SYSTEM CONTROL SPECIALIST

The system control specialist's job is probably the most overlooked of the database jobs. It is, however, one of the most important. The system control specialist is usually involved half-time in the beginning of the project, full-time during implementation, quarter-time during the first six months of operation, and then as a consultant. From time to time, significant effort may be required as major changes in the database become necessary.

The system control specialist must examine the need for audit trails from both the functional and the legal points of view. The legal requirement for audit trails may come from federal laws or from regulations promulgated by such government agencies as the Securities and Exchange Commission, the Environmental Protection Agency, and the Nuclear Regulatory Commission.

Once the requirements are determined, audit trail designs must be constructed that are complete in terms of data content, DBMS integrity, and throughput performance. The audit trails then must be implemented, tested, debugged, and documented. Finally, audit trails must be put into operation and carefully monitored for some time before they can make the transition to a maintenance state.

Backup and recovery is another critical aspect of the system control job. The system control specialist should develop tests that verify that the database being backed up is in fact good. It would be unfortunate indeed if a critical part of the database's dictionary was defective and the defective database was backed up over the last good backup. In short, there can never be too much testing when it comes to verifying database backups.

Finally, the system control specialist should construct a failsafe backup process that unloads the database data from the database into a permanent, machine-readable source format, unloads the DDL, and retains sufficient computer programs to reconstruct the database from the resultant source data and the DDL. This failsafe backup is needed in case all the normal medium backups are unrecoverable. While the alternative medium and the method of restoring this failsafe backup may not be very efficient, they are certainly better than having to re-collect the data, which may be nearly impossible anyway, if the damage occurs long after the database has been implemented.

Logical and physical database reorganization is also critically important. It ensures continued high performance in static applications and allows adjustments and evolutions of the database to occur. Databases degrade very subtly, and eventually the applications that use them often stop dead in their tracks. Carefully planned statistics must be collected and examined to detect the warning signals that demark this passage. Shortly before the database applications become comatose, database reorganization must be undertaken.

Finally, the system control specialist must be concerned about database security and privacy, which are often achieved through a combination of DBMS software capabilities, computer operations, procedures, and corporate policy about handling violations.

3.5 DOCUMENTATION AND STANDARDS

It should be clear by now that documentation and standards play more than a bit part in the database drama. In fact, the documentation of a database project plays such a large role that it must be done first. This is because it contains the rules by which all participants are governed. To attempt the database approach in developing an application without first having a complete and thorough debugged documentation of the system being developed is like trying to establish a lawful society without a constitution and a body of laws.

The documentation and standards specialist becomes the keeper of the database project implementation method. As the keeper, this person creates, understands, and instructs users on all of its aspects. Further, the keeper must monitor adherence to the standards. Any changes in standards must be made in a carefully controlled manner.

3.6 THE DBMS SPECIALIST

The importance of this position is widely recognized. However, the role is often restricted to being a DBMS guru. To make this role complete, the DBMS specialist must be given a budget to perform detailed experiments to determine, for example, the extent to which databases perform poorly due to structure degradation resulting from extensive updating or to inappropriate designs. All this information should be thoroughly documented and classified for easy recall, analysis, and refinement.

The DBMS specialist should be directly involved as a consultant in the development and operation of hotlines and as a key member of any in-house DBMS users group; and he or she should also attend regional or national group meetings for DBMS users.

Finally, the DBMS specialist should be thoroughly knowledgeable about any DBMS bugs that may have been discovered. These bugs should be verified through a standard test database, referred to the DBMS vendor, and categorized as to severity. A way to solve the bug or a technique to work around it should then be found. Finally, a bug correction date should be negotiated with the DBMS vendor. Once all this has been done, the user should be informed about progress.

3.7 THE DBA JOB DESCRIPTION

The jobs described thus far are allocated differently by different organizations. The DBA job description presented in this section consolidates all the five database specialties into one job. However, if one person were to try to perform all these roles, it is unlikely that any of them would be performed well. A suggested allocation of persons to the various aspects of the DBA job is provided in Section 3.8.

The job description is in the form prescribed by the U.S. Department of Labor. It includes an overview, detailed action-oriented job tasks, and statements about responsibility, qualifications, and the like.

Job Definition

The database administrator (DBA) assists in the creation of the logical design of the database, determines the requirements for the physical database, consults on the requirements of database interrogation languages, and designs or reviews the system control facilities necessary to keep the database in optimum condition.

In support of database operations, the DBA designs, implements, and oversees the maintenance and reporting of the metabase.

Finally, the DBA helps create and participates in the formation of proper database environment support functions such as documentation, training, hotline support, and standards.

Job Tasks

Logical Database. The DBA assists in the selection of an appropriate database domain and then coordinates the creation of an accurate database design for the domain. The design must satisfy the various needs of the users who are to contribute data and receive database reports.

Physical Database. The DBA selects a storage structure for the efficient implementation of a logical database design. This structure must be compatible with interrogation languages and must utilize as little mass storage space as is practical. In conjunction with selection of the storage structure, he or she designs an access strategy to select, retrieve, and update data in an efficient manner.

The DBA helps evaluate data quality and helps design database loading from all the previously automated applications that are being utilized with this application.

Finally, the administrator selects the method and resources to support database backup during loading and ongoing database operation.

The DBA Job Description

Interrogation. The DBA helps users of the database construct database applications. By examining the various interrogation languages, he or she determines the most appropriate language for application prototyping and then helps users select the most suitable interrogation language. The DBA assists in the development of interfaces to function between the database and canned applications such as word processing and financial modeling.

System Control. The DBA designs, creates, and maintains the appropriate audit trails, message-processing facilities, and backup and recovery procedures for database applications. These ensure that the database environment is protected against various types of loss, such as computer failures, DBMS failures, and data errors.

The DBA implements mechanisms to determine when physical database reorganization is necessary and then performs the reorganization. This involves coordinating the logical database change requests and making the changes during regularly scheduled times.

It is also the responsibility of this person to select, install, and maintain database security and privacy mechanisms that have been approved by management. The security violations log must be reviewed and the list of violations forwarded to management for action.

The DBA ensures that historical data that have been archived are retrievable under current versions of the DBMS.

Another task of the DBA is to determine which DBMS operations cannot execute concurrently and to eliminate as many of these conflicts as possible. He or she also determines which operations consume the most resources, and precludes such operations during prime time if possible.

Conducting reviews of database applications to provide recommendations for improving the operation of the application and the database is another very important task of the DBA.

The DBA supervises installation and maintenance of the DBMS and conducts tests to validate correct DBMS operation. As necessary, he or she constructs special DBMS versions to serve particular applications.

Metabase Development. The DBA creates a metabase implementation plan for the organization. Upon implementation, and subsequent to database loading, the administrator interrogates the metabase to profile the ongoing database environment.

Staffing Viewpoint

He or she advises the data administrator on development databases, production databases, maintenance projects, and the characteristics of all databases within the organization.

Documentation, Training, Hotline, and Standards. The DBA receives, reviews, catalogs and then distributes all documentation related to the DBMS. He or she keeps a log of all persons having DBMS documentation so that updates can be distributed rapidly, especially if DBMS functions are found not to be working as described.

The DBA verifies that all documentation is added to the metabase in a timely manner, distributes all database-related documentation, and produces a complete set of DBMS error reports so users can avoid the errors.

This person coordinates, designs if necessary, and attends all database training programs to ensure that students are receiving the most up-to-date material.

The DBA establishes, oversees, and reviews the operation of the DBMS hotline. All reported bugs are examined by the DBA to determine whether the user needs remedial training, or if the training needs to be changed, or if the DBMS has a bug. The DBA oversees and reviews the operation of the various database application hotlines to insure that the best advice is given the hotline's users.

He or she follows up verified DBMS errors with the vendor and determines when a DBMS correction is to be available. The DBA oversees the creation of and adherence to standards relating especially to the design, implementation, and maintenance of databases and their applications.

Interface with Other Data Processing Resources

The administrator also maintains a close working relationship with other data processing staffs and participates in solving problems that affect the database environment.

He or she prepares database in-house training seminars that relate to the effective database utilization and project specification and implementation.

This person makes presentations to indirect database support groups to describe and emphasize the impact their attention to and support of data preparation, systems programming, and computer operations has on the database environment. In addition, the DBA represents the organization to professional societies and conferences.

The DBA Job Description

Responsibility

The DBA is responsible for these important activities:

o Review of the logical database of each project.

o Transformation of the generic logical database into the one required by the DBMS.

o Specification and review of the data loading subsystem.

o Specification and review of the data update subsystem.

o Correct selection and utilization of interrogation languages.

o Correct implementation and utilization of system control facilities.

Job Knowledge

At least an undergraduate degree in mathematics, science, management science, or computer science is required for this position, with an advanced degree preferred.

More than five years experience with database and several DBMSs is necessary, and the DBA must be a competent user of the operating systems under which the DBMS resides. He or she also must have several years' experience with large-scale information systems. The DBA must have a demonstrated capability to plan and manage large projects.

Mental Application

The DBA must be alert to the "big picture" as well as to small details in order to evaluate events and allocate resources according to the relative importance and size of the problem.

He or she must be able to plan and predict resources required to accomplish goals. Finally, this person must gain the cooperation and support of database application users.

Dexterity and Accuracy

The DBA must be able to communicate effectively in order to handle meetings in which there may be significant conflicts and problems, and must be able to assess an issue and propose acceptable solutions.

3.8 STAFF ALLOCATION

Figure 3.1 presents a matrix that indicates the type, location, and number of staff required for both the database project and the centralized DBA organization that should be involved in a database project.

NUMBER	RESPONSIBILITY	LOCATION
1 per project	Database specialist	Database Project Staff
1 per project	Interrogation specialist	
1 per project	Data loading	
1 per project	Data update	
2 per project	Functional user staff	
1 DBA group	Documentation and standards	DBA Centralized Staff
1 DBA group	Systems Control	
1 per DBMS	DBMS	

Figure 3.1   Database Project Staff & Allocation

The size of the centralized DBA staff can often remain reasonably small; it is determined only by the number of projects to which the staff are consultants and the number of different operational DBMSs.

The number of staff members needed for a given database project ranges from a minimum of seven to a number large enough to cover all the project's requirements. The database specialist on the project could report either to the project's department or to the centralized DBA staff. The decision should be made on the basis of the ownership of the database projects. If all the projects are from one department, then it is logical that the database specialist report to that department. If the projects are from different departments, then the database specialist should work for the DBA group, since no one department could justify the full-time job.

The project's staff consists of one database specialist, two or three functional users, two data processing professionals for the data loading and update subsystems, and one data processing professional for each major interrogation subsystem. The database specialist draws knowledge mainly from functional staff assigned to the project. The functional users can revert to their previous duties once the major database design work is accomplished.

3.9 STAFF SUMMARY

Since a database project is different from a traditional data processing project, the staffing required to undertake it is also different. Five different types of skilled persons should be represented in a database administration (DBA) group.

A database specialist is needed to help functional users create a complete database design. An interrogation specialist is needed to assist users select and then utilize the most appropriate DBMS access language for loading, update, and retrieval. A system control specialist is needed to research, design, and implement the proper protections, safeguards, and optimizations; and to verify that these elements are present in each database application. A documentation and standards specialist is needed to ensure that applications are implemented in a consistent and uniform manner to enhance data and program interchange. Finally, a DBMS specialist is needed to install, test, configure, and fix the DBMS, and to ensure that applications are created that utilize the DBMS in the most efficient manner.

The jobs described in this chapter are allocated differently within different organizations. The DBA job description presented above consolidates all the five database specialities into one job. Remember, however, that if one person were to try to perform all these roles, it is unlikely that any of them would be performed well.

Experience is critical to high-quality staff performance. Experience cannot be acquired from training courses alone; it must be developed through a combination of failures and successes. Failure, if those involved are allowed to survive, is the best teacher of all. The person knows not only the wrong way but also the right way. The best way to reduce the expense of a colossal failure is to create a small, well-engineered failure.

Staffing Viewpoint

This can be done through carefully planned workshops that involve real projects and real deadlines--but not in mission-critical areas.

3.10 REVIEW QUESTIONS

1. List the areas that need to be staffed with skilled personnel when implementing a database project.

2. Why is it important to have a qualified database area specialist?

3. During application implementation, what is a critical duty of the database specialist?

4. How does the interrogation specialist reflect the overall success of a database project?

5. Which is the most overlooked specialist in the database field? What are this specialist's primary responsibilities and duties?

6. Which type of specialist should oversee and guide the users of a database?

7. What prerequisite is critical to high quality staff performance?

8. What role does the DBMS specialist play during the actual use of a database?

9. What is the minimum number of people needed to run an efficient database system?

10. Under what conditions should the database specialist report to the DBA group or to the functional area?

4 Database and Data Administration

Data administration (DA), data resource administration (DRA), data resource management (DRM), and information resource management (IRM) are four synonyms for essentially the same high-level organizational function. In general, data administration should be a department that reports directly to the head of the organization. This department should have responsibility for defining the information requirements of each functional component of the organization.

DA should be the coordinating group for the definition of the information content, meaning, and intrinsic value of all permanent data within the organization. In short, this group is responsible for the organization's data semantics. These semantics enable different suborganizations to share data and thus reduce work. DA should further ensure that the different databases are compatible enough to be accessed by programs or procedures that have a demonstrated need for access. Figure 1.2 illustrates the trade-offs relating to the centralization of semantics.

Finally, to avoid any chance of a fatal data loss, the DA group should institute procedures to guarantee the overall integrity, reliability, and relatability of all data within the organization as a whole.

To accomplish all these missions, data administration must certainly have database administration as one of its subordinate organizations. Ideally, word processing, data communications, and data processing should also be within data administration.

The data administration group needs to have its products, projects, and progress constantly reviewed by a user committee. That committee is discussed at the end of this chapter.

4.2 WORD PROCESSING

Word processing is the capture, playback, and modification of strings of text. The several types of systems are either wholly self-contained or subordinate units of a bigger machine. The self-contained systems are usually not able to communicate with other environments. A major exception to this generalization is the microcomputer, which contains a word processing software package. While its sophistication is directly related to the quality of the software, it offers a more generalized set of capabilities because it is first a computer.

The multi-station systems are generally superior to the self-contained word processors because they are likely to have more storage, faster printers, and more sophisticated capabilities for file sharing and other functions.

There is a growing realization that there is not much difference between data processing and word processing. Evidence of this realization is the merger of the ANSI committees X3 (Computers) and X4 (Office Equipment), with X3 as the survivor.

The relationship of word processing to database is very clear. It is a source of inferential data about a subject that might belong in a database. The document produced by a word processing exercise can also be the destination of data selected from a database by a natural language interrogation.

For example, a matrix report containing the current names and profit-and-loss ratios for the top 15 companies selling microprocessors in China could be automatically collated into a letter created by a secretary.

Data administration should certainly promote the capabilities and control the extent of word processing, because so much corporate effort is expended in both internal and external communications. Electronic messages are much cheaper than paper, and word processing is a method of presenting contextually bound messages rather than bursts of uninterpreted facts. The most critical aspect of word processing is whether the text can be communicated to others and combined into standard data processing reports.

4.3 DATA COMMUNICATIONS

Data communications embraces all the hardware and software necessary to transmit data from user to user via a computer, from user to computer, computer to user, and computer to computer.

This field is receiving great attention from vendors. Many new products have been released or announced, especially since IBM and AT&T have broadened their product lines dramatically in this area.

For example, AT&T has already developed commercial computers, and IBM has developed communications systems. IBM now has office communications systems that store voice messages and make telephone calls to a list of individuals until all are contacted. AT&T and other companies have put microprocessors in their communications equipment to enhance reliability and to expand services. In Texas, AT&T has a time-sharing service for home shopping, news, research, and other purposes.

Data communications make database operations possible. In the early stages of development, the database environment was characterized by multiple batch jobs in the computer, but now database operations involve extensive communications of interrelated data among remote stations.

4.4 DATA PROCESSING

Data processing, whether performed by a collection of large mainframes, minicomputers, microcomputers, or combinations of these, should come under the management and control of data administration rather than any functional unit of the corporation, such as finance or research and development. This is simply because data processing serves all functional units. Thus, to have it under the control of one functional unit would place all other units in a less than equal relationship with the unit controlling it.

With the advent of very sophisticated DBMSs--systems with a large number of interrogation languages, static and dynamic relationship capabilities, multithreaded update, solid security, and the like--the requirement to have a centralized data processing design, implementation, and maintenance staff is inappropriately authoritarian and likely to perpetuate an environment in which the quantity of backlogged system changes accelerates. The inverse situation is no more acceptable, however. If there were one computer, one policy, and one set of updates for each person, surely chaos or anarchy would result. The right-hand column of Figure 1.2 provides answers to critical questions when data anarchy reigns.

What is needed is a balance between centralized control of the critical aspects of a computer system and decentralized opportunity to create different uses of data that has a high degree of integrity (for a change). The database approach to data processing allows for just such a balance. There is a real need for a centralized and methodical process of defining both the data that is to be stored in the database and the centralized and critical process of data loading and data update. These two centralized processes must of course be accomplished with the support and guidance of the functional users.

Once the database is "up," the process of defining, implementing, and maintaining reports for the database can be carried out in a decentralized way by the users, for they know best the current and future needs.

4.5 THE DATA ADMINISTRATION COMMITTEE

The data administration committee needs to be instituted to make the data administration department responsive to the needs of the corporation. Without such a committee, the DA department could easily become the most powerful corporate group.

The committee should have a chairman and both standing and ad hoc committees to conduct whatever studies are appropriate. These projects should deal with at least the following areas:

o   Feasibility studies for new hardware and software.

o   Cost-benefit studies on the implementation of new methods and techniques.

o   Review of user community education.

o   Review and management of the multiple user-department management information system's implementation schedules.

o   Definition of data maintenance support contracts.

o   Resolution of security breaches.

o   Enforcement of integrity policies.

o   Production of quality documentation.

o   Resolution of significant problems.

4.6 DATA ADMINISTRATION SUMMARY

Data administration is the manifestation of a realized database environment that exists when the corporation recognizes the importance of data and realizes value from all the resources it expends on data collection, storage, and dissemination. Traditionally, the ratio of resource expenditures for these three factors is probably 100 to 100 to 1. The reason dissemination is so low is that data is typically collected for only one purpose, and to use it for any other purpose is very difficult and its value is highly suspect.

If data were collected using a database approach, the ratios would probably be 1 to 1 to 100. This is because the data is collected under a constant set of publicly recognized policies and stored in formats that allow many uses. The face value of the data would therefore be very high. It would be used over and over, first for controlling the present, then for understanding the past, and finally for forecasting the requirements of strategic business needs far into the future.

Constancy of data interpretation and usage require cooperation among all the data providers. While they need to maintain their individuality as important contributors, they also need to understand the value of standardization and consistency. The data administration committee, acting as a sort of board of governors, facilitates this cooperation.

4.7 REVIEW QUESTIONS

1. What is the relationship between word processing and database?

2. State the major functions of data administration.

Database and Data Administration

3. What are the principal aspects and functions of data communications?

4. Why is it a good idea for the data processing department to be under the management of data administration?

5. What are the main functions and responsibilities of the data administration committee?

6. Describe typical studies that would be under the direction of the data administration committee.

7. Devise a strategy for introducing data administration within an organization that has a centralized DP organization under accounting. Devise a counter-strategy to defeat this.

8. Devise a strategy to implement effective data administration within an organization that currently has a minicomputer for each department. Devise a counter-strategy to defeat this.

9. Describe the five most useful and the five least useful activities in which a data administration department can engage.

5 The Project Viewpoint

5.1 CRITICAL PROJECT DIFFERENCES

The database approach to system design is different from the traditional approach in six significant ways. First, at the center of the database approach are databases, not reports. A database should never be designed to satisfy the needs of computer reports. It should be designed to enhance the orderly process of organizational decision making in some well-bounded area. The database thus becomes a computer-based model of that business area. Because it is a natural model, the fundamental design of the model lasts as long as the fundamental design of the business.

Second, the database is designed by users within the business. Since they know the organization best, they are uniquely qualified to design the database. The resultant design is a complete, user-defined, corporate-policy-based specification of the organization in which it resides. If it is correct, it is obviously correct. If it is wrong, it is obviously wrong. It cannot look right and be wrong, nor can it look wrong and be right. A database design is not a feat of technology, it is the practice of common sense. In short, if the design does not make common sense, it makes no sense at all.

Third, if the developer of a database project has access to a dynamic DBMS, then the database approach can greatly benefit from the building of a prototype of the entire database system during the first phase of the project. With a dynamic DBMS, this can be accomplished in a few weeks. When this prototype is demonstrated to and employed by the users, necessary design changes become obvious. Since the prototype takes only weeks to create, changes to it take only days. The revised prototype is then demonstrated. This cycle of prototyping continues until the system design becomes quiescent. Then, and only then, is it time to proceed with the implementation of the operational specification.

Fourth, computer-generated reports assume their rightful stature: very low. This is because the goal of a database project is the design and implementation of the database. Only after the database has been designed and its physical database and system control components fully implemented is it time to begin work on the interrogation modules (reports).

Because report modules are not part of the database project's critical path, they can come and go without disturbing the design or operation of the database.

Because many DBMSs have multiple interrogation languages, users are able to avail themselves of nontechnical query languages, semitechnical procedure-oriented languages, report writers, and very complex compiler languages such as COBOL and FORTRAN.

This fourth difference demonstrates an important dissimilarity between traditional systems and systems designed through the database approach. The traditional system design is today's use of data, whereas the database approach to system design is focused on the fundamental business policies that dictate data organization and structure. The former is like building a system on a foundation of shifting sands; the latter is like building on time-tested granite.

Fifth, the traditional approach requires the expenditure of about 85 percent of all the money and time allocated for system development before the design can be demonstrated. Changes required at that point are both expensive and time-consuming. Each change postpones the system delivery date.

The database approach, on the other hand, encourages the creation of design hypotheses and changes before system implementation. Only when the design becomes quiescent should implementation be considered. At that time, the system's delivery date can be predicted with confidence for these reasons:

o   The design has already been shown to be correct.

o It is left to the user to write all or most of the ongoing interrogation subsystems using any of the DBMS language alternatives.

The sixth difference is in system maintenance. The database is designed from a foundation of organizational knowledge; thus, changes to it are minor. Major changes occur only when the database has not been correctly designed initially or when there is a fundamental change in the nature of the business. The first can be prevented; the second seldom occurs. Reports do change, but since they are not a critical part of the database system, the effect of such changes is not significant. And with the advent of sophisticated natural languages, old reports can be modified easily and new reports can be constructed in a few hours. In short, maintenance is part of the database approach to system design; because of this, changes become evolutions of systems, not revolutions.

5.2 PROJECT PHASES

The database project is completed in three main phases. Figure 5.1 presents these phases and the level of effort expended in each.

The first phase, conceptual specification, consists of activities in each of the four database parts: logical, physical, interrogation, and system control. In the logical database component, the rules that define the database's integrity are developed. This collection of rules is called the data integrity model. In the physical database, the rules that define acceptable data transformations are completely specified. This collection of rules is called the data transformation model. Also addressed, but in a minor way, is the remainder of the physical database, interrogation and system control. At the end of this phase, the database is designed and the remainder of the project is in conceptual specification form. Figure 5.2 presents the principal activities and the products of this phase.

The amount of work required in the conceptual specification phase is considerable. This is true for all database projects, regardless of the DBMS employed. It should never be supposed that this work is not needed when the project is intending to use a dynamic DBMS rather than a static one, because these activities are even more important with a dynamic DBMS. Most dynamic DBMSs offer interrecord integrity only through user-written programs, rather than centrally through schemata. This means that all the data integrity rules and the data transformation rules must be specified correctly and without variance in all programs. That's a lot of work.

	DATABASE PROJECT COMPONENTS			
DATABASE PROJECT PHASE	LOGICAL DATABASE	PHYSICAL DATABASE	INTERRO-GATION	SYSTEM CONTROL
CONCEPTUAL SPECIFI-CATION	Significant effort	Little or no effort	Basic sketches only	Data gathering to make fundamental decisions
IMPLEMEN-TATION	Finalized designs & all details	Significant effort, R&D, testing, etc.	Traditional design, test debug and documenta-tion	Significant effort for design, implementa-tion & test
PRODUCTION and ADMINIS-TRATION	Ongoing maintenance	Minor adjustments	Typical new applications & main-tenance	Significant command & control effort & activities

Figure 5.1   Relationship between Phases and Components in Terms of Effort

The second major phase, implementation, concentrates on transforming the conceptual specifications into computer code and procedures, both manual and automated, to load and update the database and to protect it through system control capabilities. Once completed, the database becomes operational. Interrogation is purposely downplayed because it is not a critical part of database. The data integrity model is transformed into the schema data definition language (DDL) and data integrity procedures that reside in the schema or update programs. The data transformation model becomes the major portion of the loading and data update subsystems. Figure 5.3 presents the main activities and the products of this phase.

The third major phase, production and administration, is ongoing; that is, it is concerned with the actual operation and administration of the database environment. The activities in this phase are first directed to the development of database interrogation subsystems and then toward performance optimization, design evolution, and maintenance of the four database components. Figure 5.4 presents the major activities and the principal products of this phase.

Additional activities associated with each of these phases are presented in the next three chapters.

5.3 PROJECT SCHEDULES AND STAFF ALLOCATION

The conceptual specification phase should not last much more than six months. The database specialist is the principal technical adviser during this phase. The majority of the personnel must be from the functional area so that the database can be designed to model the real requirements, not just those that produce efficient data processing.

DATABASE COMPONENTS			
LOGICAL DATABASE	PHYSICAL DATABASE	INTERRO- GATION	SYSTEM CONTROL
Graphic specification	Preliminary analysis	Minimum reporting requirements	Data gathering
Object formation	Operation formation		
Element formation	DBMS partitions		
Data structures			
Data integrity rule formation			
Model validation			
Preliminary transformation			

Figure 5.2   Activities in the Conceptual Specification Phase

63

The Project Viewpoint

At the end of the conceptual phase, the system control specialist should be involved for a short time to conceptually specify the requirements for audit trails, other critical system control components, DBMS selection and procurement, and equipment selection and installation. In addition to the system control specialist, the DBMS specialist can be employed to construct a preliminary transformation of the database from its logical DBMS-independent form to that required by the DBMS.

The implementation phase usually lasts from 6 to 18 months, depending on the complexity of the system being created, the sophistication of the DBMS employed, the critical nature of the application, and the amount and quality of the data that has to be collected or transformed during database loading.

DATABASE PROJECT COMPONENTS			
LOGICAL DATABASE	PHYSICAL DATABASE	INTERRO-GATION	SYSTEM CONTROL
Refined schema	Design of storage structure	Designs, listings, run instructions of required interrogations	Specifications of audit trails
	Specification of of all access strategies	Testing systems and data	Test backup and recovery
	Design, etc. of data loading subsystem	Inputs, outputs, workfile specifications	Specifications of security and privacy
	Design, etc., of data update subsystem	Preliminary estimates	Messages
	Creation of all database backup designs and resource consumption estimates		System resource consumption estimates

Figure 5.3 Activities in the Implementation Phase

Project Schedules and Staff Allocation

During the implementation phase, a majority of the data-base specialists are involved. The database specialist oversees the transformation of the database design to ensure that it is not compromised. The interrogation specialists are busy creating the data loading and update subsystems. The system control specialist is developing all the critical protection and control software and procedures. The DBMS specialist is determining the most efficient way to engineer the DBMS to make the various project subsystems perform optimally. The standards and documentation specialist is ensuring that the methods and documentation are produced correctly and in a timely manner. Finally, the functional users are constantly being involved to ensure that the system is being developed according to their conceptual specification.

The last phase, production and administration, is ongoing. It includes an initial shakedown period of about three months. During this time, all the subsystems are thoroughly tested to remove any integration problems that may still exist. Training occurs during this period, and all the documentation is finalized.

DATABASE PROJECT COMPONENTS			
LOGICAL DATABASE	PHYSICAL DATABASE	INTERRO-GATION	SYSTEM CONTROL
Change requests	Revision of all physical estimates	Updates of resource estimates	Updated resource estimates
	Update proce-cedures for backups	Updates of all documentation	Changes and new facilities
	Optimization of storage structrure	Program modifications	Schedule adjustments
		Schedule adjustments	Optimization and special reports

Figure 5.4   Activities in the Production and Administration Phase

Subsequent to this initial period, all the specialists are involved as needed to implement modifications to the system. Figure 5.5 illustrates the length of time for each phase and the personnel primarily involved in each. Figure 5.6 indicates the level of effort for each of the phases.

5.4   THE METABASE

A tremendous amount of paper is produced during the database project. If it is left as paper, its administration and maintenance could well bury the entire process.

The metabase is a database application that contains all the data about the database project. The record types contained in the metabase relate directly to the three phases of the data-base project. If the metabase design or one similar to it is implemented, the whole process of data administration can be greatly streamlined. The metabase helps in these important areas:

   o   Management has a tool to better organize, con-
         trol, and schedule the scarce resources required
         to build an information system.

PHASE	LENGTH	PERSONNEL
Conceptual specification	4-8 months	Database specialist Functional users System control specialist
Implementation	6-18 months	DBMS specialist Database specialist Interrogation specialist System control specialist Standards and documenta- tion specialist
Production and administration	3 months - system life	Interrogation specialist (and, as neeaed) Database specialist Interrogation specialist System control specialist Standards and documenta- tion specialist

Figure 5.5   Personnel Involvement and Time Spans for Project Phases

   o   Database administration has a well-organized
         storehouse of information about past database
         efforts that can be used during the design of
         new databases.

The Metabase

o A metabase allows for storage of data definitions and policies, which will produce greater consistency throughout an organization.

o Database project estimates are more accurate, as the metabase allows evaluation of past efforts.

o Application development can be enhanced through the utilization of prior work that has been implemented in a generalized way. The metabase should contain descriptions of each computer module, which can be examined and utilized as appropriate.

DATABASE PROJECT PHASE	DATABASE COMPONENT			
	LOGICAL	PHYSICAL	INTERRO-GATION	SYSTEM CONTROL
	PERCENTAGE WITHIN PHASE			
CONCEPTUAL SPECIFICATION	70%	10%	10%	10%
IMPLEMENTA-TION	10%	35%	20%	35%
PRODUCTION AND ADMINISTRA TION	10%	15%	50%	25%
	PERCENT OVER ALL PHASES			
	30%	20%	27%	23%

Figure 5.6   Percentage Distribution of Effort by Project Phase

o Proposed modifications to a database can be assessed through access to the metabase, which contains the identification of all affected programs, procedures, policies, and rules.

o Operations can benefit from the data contained in the metabase, as it permits the generation of resource requirement statistics and projections of the impact of new systems.

The message is simple. Designing and installing the metabase application is critical to the long-range success of database.

5.5 PROJECT SUMMARY

The database project should be designed to include only those activities critical to the success of database. In the conceptual specification phase, activities are centered primarily on the database design, as it must be completed before any other activity can begin.

The implementation phase consists primarily of the activities required to load and update the database and those required to protect it from destruction or loss. At the end of the implementation phase, the database project could be considered as complete.

The production and administration phase includes the ongoing development of reporting subsystems and whatever changes to the database might be required.

The next three chapters present a more detailed account of the three phases of the database project.

5.6 REVIEW QUESTIONS

1.   Which members of an organization have a unique ability to organize the database in the most functionally efficient manner? Why?

2.   Which members of an organization have a unique ability to organize the database in the most computer efficient manner? Why?

3.   Why, in a database system, are computer-generated reports of lesser importance than the basic design of the database?

4.   What is the major difference between the traditional data processing environment and the database approach?

5.   Justify the cost of the database approach as compared to the cost of the traditional approach.

Review Questions

6. What happens during the conceptual specification phase of the database project? What is done during this phase with regard to the physical database?

7. Name and describe the major activities constituting the implementation phase.

8. What is the final phase of a database project? What are its major activities and its principal products? When is this phase complete?

9. How much time should be allocated for the implementation of each phase of a database project? Why not less? Why not more?

10. What is a metabase? Why is it important? List the ways in which it assists in the daily operation of a database.

6 The Conceptual Specification Phase

The conceptual specification phase of the database project consists of activities in each of the four components: logical, physical, interrogation, and systems control. The main emphasis in this phase is on the logical database. Attention is paid to the other components only for the purpose of initial analysis and specification.

6.1 DATABASE STATES

A database can be viewed as being in either of two states: at-rest or in-motion. In the at-rest state, updating is not occurring. In the in-motion state, updating is occurring. During either state, one must be able to determine the quality of the database. In the at-rest state, this is accomplished through the implied execution of data integrity and consistency rules. The totality of these rules is called the data integrity model.

During the in-motion state, data transformation for either update or reporting must follow certain rules, but some of the at-rest rules may be suspended. The in-motion rules are called data transformation rules. The totality of these rules is called the data transformation model.

When these two models are transformed to meet the requirements of a particular DBMS, the data integrity model is mapped principally into the DBMS's allowable data model, the schema-based data integrity statements, and possibly the computer code in the data load and data update subsystems. The

71

data transformation model is mapped completely into the data update subsystem.

6.2 DATABASE DOMAIN AND SCHEMATIC

The first step in the definition of both the data integrity and the data transformation models is creation of the database domain. It is a statement of the fundamental goal or objective of the database project. This half-page or less statement clearly states both the real value of the database system in terms of modified behaviors and the major sources and uses of data.

The database domain is used as the basis of the data integrity model and the data transformation model. Figure 6.1 presents an example of a database domain.

The sales and marketing database is to contain accurate and timely data about the company, its products, product specifications, prices, salesmen, customers' contracts and their orders. The system is to contain data on all sales, so that marketing plans can be formulated for company customers.

Figure 6.1   Database Domain

Once the database domain has been drafted and approved, a schematic of the entire database system can be created to illustrate the interaction among major system components. Figure 6.2 illustrates a system schematic. The symbolism used follows the ANSI standard for flow charting templates, except for the diamond, which is used to designate interaction between components rather than decision making. For example, the diamond GENERATES means that the ORDERs and CUSTOMER data are utilized by the REPORT subsystem to generate REPORTs. The diagrams generally name the main data types without regard to whether the data belong to one, a few, or many databases.

The database domain statement and the database system schematic are the most critical starting points for the database project. These serve as boundary markers that enable subsequent analysis and specification to remain focused.

6.3 LOGICAL DATABASE SPECIFICATION

The logical database segment of this phase is by far the largest activity. Its goal is to develop the data integrity model. To define this model, the following items must be specified:

o Entity-relationship diagram

o Objects

o Elements

o Data structures

o Data integrity rules

The process of database design is not at all casual. It is rigorous. The product is a comprehensive representation of corporate policy in the area covered by the database. The specification of the database builds the foundation upon which all other database activities are built. These other activities include data loading, data update, interrogation, and system control.

This logical database foundation includes an entity relationship diagram of the database, specifications for each object and element, and specifications for the integrity rules that govern their interaction.

Taken together, these define the complete database integrity model. An example of an entity-relationship diagram and examples of each of the specification types are illustrated in Figures 6.3 to 6.6.

The Entity-Relationship Diagram

The purpose of the entity-relationship (E-R) diagram is to create an initial view of the scope and domain of the database. It is therefore derived from the database domain.

The entity-relationship diagram shows the main data groupings (entities) as squares and a generalized version of the principal major actions (relationships) as diamonds. The diamonds represent generalized mechanisms of relationship among two or more data groupings.

Many benefits are derived from these diagrams; one of them is implementation independence. The E-R diagram is not oriented to any data model or even to any method of database or data processing implementation. It is merely a graphic representation of the database domain that can be easily read and understood. An example of an entity-relationship diagram is given in Figure 6.3.

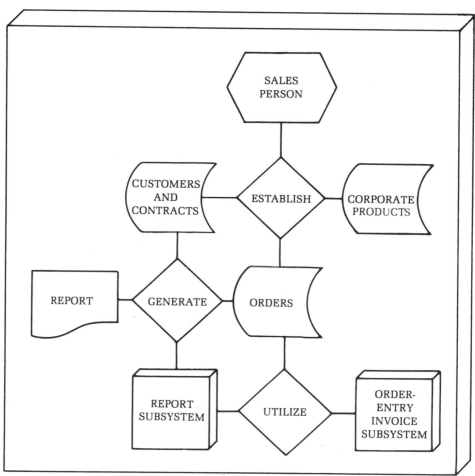

Figure 6.2 Database System Schematic

Logical Database Specification

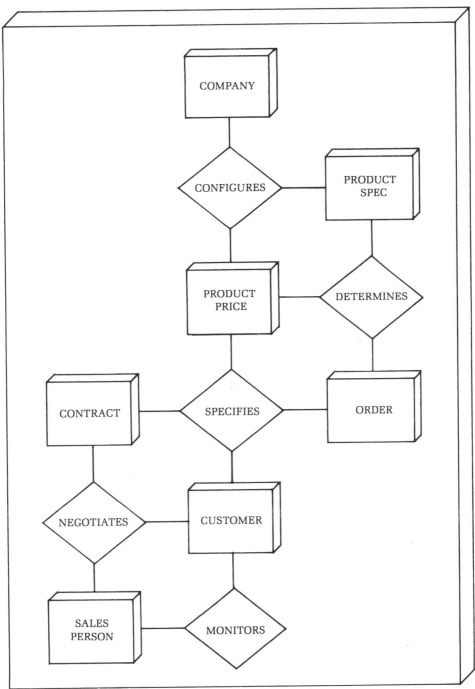

Fig. 6.3 Sales and Marketing Entity-Relationship Diagram

COMPONENT: OBJECT
NAME: CONTRACT

PURPOSE:
- A contract is an agreement between the company and the customer.
- A contract allows orders to be entered by a customer.
- A contract is sold by a salesperson.

PROPERTIES:
- Critical dates
- Identification data
- Pricing and cost data
- Summary order information
- Discount rates

DATA STRUCTURE:
- Primary key: contract number
- Attributes:
  Contract-Id, numeric
  Date signed, date
  Customer name, text
  Customer address, text
  Customer phone, numeric
  Minimum cost, numeric
  Maximum cost, numeric
  Total number of orders, numeric
  Total order cost, numeric
  Salesperson-Id, numeric

OBJECT INTEGRITY RULES:
- All fields must be valued.
- Total number of orders must be at least one.
- Total order cost must be greater than zero.
- Salesperson must be or have been employed by company at time contract is signed.

Figure 6.4 Contract Object Specification

```
COMPONENT:      DATA ELEMENT

      NAME:     CONTRACT ID

 DEFINITION:    • A contract number is a unique number assigned by
                  accounting.

DATA CONTENT:   • Value range of the contract is 1 to 99,999.

DATA STRUCTURE: • Type is decimal with no decimal places.
```

Figure 6.5   Element Specification

The process of creating an entity-relationship diagram is entirely functional, rather than technical. When the functional knowledge of the designers greatly overshadows the technical, the diagram is typically excellent and very easy to construct. But, when the technical knowledge of the designers greatly overshadows the functional, the diagram is often inaccurate, and difficult to construct.

Once the entity-relationship diagram is constructed, the domain of the database is complete. From this point on, the database's design is a matter of detailing and justifying. If really new entities emerge during subsequent processes, then either the initial E-R diagram was incorrect or the problem has changed. In a general sense, the E-R diagram, once correctly drawn, remains valid throughout the life of the database.

Object Specification

The step that naturally follows the creation of the E-R diagram is the definition of database objects. In a well-designed database, each object represents a complete policy statement. It can stand on its own.

The complete specification of an object includes descriptions of its purpose, properties, data structures, and data integrity rules. The object's purpose and properties are created when the object is initially defined. The data structures and data integrity rules are defined later in the logical database.

```
COMPONENT:   DATA INTEGRITY RULE

     NAME:   CONTRACT-ORDER

    OWNER:   CONTRACT

   MEMBER:   ORDER

    RULES:   • For each contract, there must be orders that are
               entered during the term of contract.

             • No contract can exist without at least one order.

             • For each order there must be a contract.

             • No order can belong to more than one contract.

             • The order delivery date must not be after the
               contract termination date.
```

Figure 6.6   Contract-Order Interobject Integrity Rule

When the characteristics of an object have been publicly analyzed, defined, and agreed upon, there can be no doubt about its purpose and exact role. Without such a definitional consensus, only a few will know the "truth," and in time their view of that will change. The result is a slow disintegration of the database. An example of an object is contained in Figure 6.4.

When an object is rigorously defined through the examination of policy, some of the entities in the E-R diagram may disappear. There are two reasons for this. First, no one can really define a role or purpose for the object, except, of course, the Great High Lord, Tradition. Second, an entity may be just a data element. In either case, an adjustment to the E-R diagram should be made.

Element Specifications

A natural successor to definition of the object is definition of the data element. It would be simple just to examine the properties of the object and enumerate the most appropriate set of data elements. That, however, is not the safe way.

Logical Database Specification

Data elements must be defined in their own right. Organizations have gone to great lengths to collect massive amounts of data. Each data element in these collections must be examined and categorized within a data dictionary. The retention of these must be based squarely on policy. When this is done, each data element (like each object) has a policy-based definition, a content description, a data structure, and any data integrity rules that relate to the element. An example of a specified element is found in Figure 6.5.

Data Structures

The process of building data structures consists of assigning elements to objects and creating an object graphic that illustrates the final product. Once all the data elements have been examined and stored in the dictionary, the process of assigning data elements to objects can begin. An element is assigned to an object only if it serves as a partial descriptor of that object. An indication of that is contained in the properties section of the object specification.

It is possible that an element will surface from the dictionary that properly belongs to the object but has not had its category included in the object's properties section. In such a case, the data dictionary of policy-based data elements serves as a check on the completeness of the object definition.

The object definition serves further as a check on the list of data elements contained in the dictionary. If a data category is contained in the object specification and there are no data elements in the dictionary inventory, then not only must the data element be established, but the data dictionary must also be updated.

Natural collections of multiple-occurring elements are grouped together to form subordinate structures. Each of these structures is then examined to see if it is in third normal form; that is, in a structure whose segments have the following characteristics:

o All elements are single valued. No elements are like nicknames or dependents.

o The segment's data elements are uniquely accessible by a single data element's value (primary key) that is contained in the segment.

o All elements depend only on the primary key element for their meaning, not on any other element.

The purpose of third normal form structure is to achieve single-purpose data segments that can be selected, modified, and updated unambiguously. If all the prior database design steps have been performed correctly, the segment will probably already be in this form. If it is not, and if the process of arriving at third normal form causes major disruptions to the object's structure, then an error has been made in one or more of the prior steps. Validating that the object's segments are in third normal form is another of the check steps in the database design process.

The process of forcing object type structures into third normal form produces an additional benefit. All data elements that are not truly a part of the object type are extracted from the object and set aside. The object is then free from all dependencies on other object types.

In the next step, data integrity rule specification, if any of these set-aside dependencies are in fact legitimate, then they are collated back in, along with any other relationships. All the dependencies are recorded as interobject data integrity rules.

The final step in creating data structures is the development of an object graphic. It depicts the results of creating structures of related objects. Figure 6.7 illustrates such a diagram for the customer management database. An arrow indicates a one-to-many relationship. For example, a CUSTOMER has many CONTRACTS.

Database integrity is built on a foundation of object type integrity, which in turn can only be built on data element integrity.

Data Integrity Rules

An integrity rule is a legalistic expression of a relationship between the specification of a type and its data instances, or between different instances of data. Included in the scope of type are elements, relationships, and records.

An example of an element-type data-integrity rule might be if a data element SALARY is defined as numeric, then there is an implied integrity rule that no "letters" be allowed as valid values. When data integrity rules are intra-object, they are defined within the object's specification.

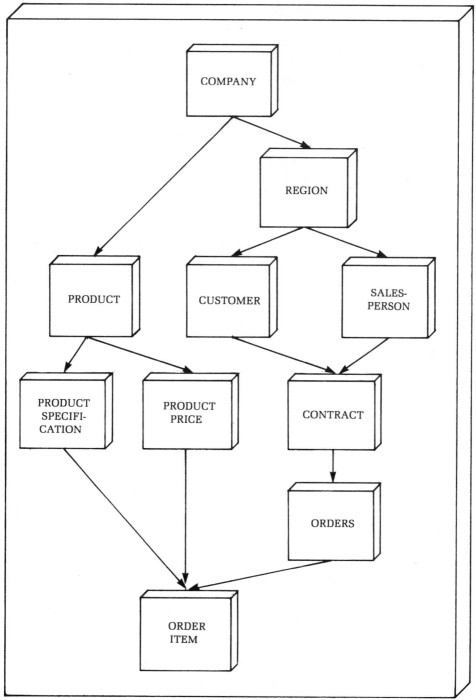

Figure 6.7   Sales and Marketing Object Graphic

The Conceptual Specification Phase

An example of a data-integrity rule relating to different instances of data might be if the SALARY of a department were required to be the sum of the salaries of that department's employees. The integrity rule in the database for this example then, is first, that no salary can contain letters, and second, that the department salary must be equal to the sum of the employees' salaries.

Data-integrity rules should specify all possible situations in which data elements semantically restrict their values, or when there are relationships between data elements in the same or different objects, or when there are relationships between objects. Obviously then, since every database consists of many object types, there are several times more data integrity rules than defined objects.

The first indication of a data-integrity rule or relationship is in the entity-relationship diagram (Figure 6.1). Each diamond represents a macro relationship. As the database specification becomes more refined, these macro relationships become a series of micro relationships. For the purposes of this book, the use of the word "relationship" is equivalent to "data-integrity rule."

Each data integrity rule has a strict form. Each must include a definition, and a clear, unambiguous set of rules that must be met before the conditions it represents are satisfied. Figure 6.6 presents the specification of a data-integrity rule.

In addition to relationships that bind together records of the same or different types, some of the explicitly defined relationships describe data duplicated in different objects, data derived or summarized from other objects, and data constrained by values in other objects. Finally, relationships or data-integrity rules are needed to document the instances of objects that are conditioned on the instances of other objects. For example, a dependent record describing the nature of an employee's handicap is conditioned on the instance of the value contained in the data element: HANDICAP-CODE.

Each of these types of relationships, along with those for the objects and elements, must be documented in the database specification. Taken together, these data-integrity rules define the dimensions of data integrity and consistency that must be present when the database is in the at-rest state.

The data integrity rules that are intra-object are recorded within the object's definition, while those that are inter-object must be recorded in the data integrity rule specification section. Without rigorous and complete data integrity rule specification, there can only be database disintegration.

82

Logical Database Specification

Logical Database Summary

The logical database within the context of the conceptual specification is the complete codification of all the policies that are to exist in the database. It is founded initially on the domain, next on the objects existing within the domain, then on the elements within the objects, and finally on the rules that bind the records together with integrity. Clearly this process is both top-down and founded squarely on functional requirements.

Benefits of the Design Process

The design process just described has the following significant benefits, which also serve to answer often-heard objections to implemented data processing systems:

o The functional users are the database designers. It is their knowledge of the actual workings os the organization that becomes the database's design. Consequently, it cannot ever be said that the database does not fulfill user needs.

o The entire process is founded on the inherent sensibility of the subject matter, rather than on computer hardware or software efficiencies. Consequently, it cannot ever be said that the illogic of a system is due to the computer.

o The database design can easily be developed into a prototype to be demonstrated to end users well before any significant sums are expended on implementation. Consequently, it cannot ever be said that changes were not allowed in an attempt to make the system useful.

o The details of the actual DBMS to be used during implementation are not brought into the picture until the very end of the design process. Consequently, the application's architecture--having been firmly established--is the benchmark against which DBMS implementations of the application are judged rather than against computer efficiencies.

6.4 PHYSICAL DATABASE SPECIFICATION

The conceptual specification of the physical database provides needed information for determining the size and number of databases, the access strategy that must be employed, a preliminary understanding of the data loading requirements, and the complete specification of all the data transformations that are to occur while the database is in-motion to accomplish updates. All these physical database components must be analyzed and specified to provide a complete picture of the proposed database application.

The Data Loading Subsystem

Before any real work can begin on the specification of the data loading subsystem, the quality level of the data that are to be incorporated into the database must be determined. A study should be made to identify the issues surrounding this important subject. For example, there may be ten different sex codes in the same source of data or from ten different sources.

Such analyses must be made of each and every data source. In examining a data source, if data quality policies have been established, but data values are not in conformance with these policies, the persons who carried out these policies must be found and the data variances corrected; otherwise, the new database will disintegrate shortly after it becomes operational.

If the database is to be an amalgamation of data from many different sources, the data policies established are very likely to be at variance with those already in existence. In such a case, meetings must be held in which compromise and agreement can be achieved. Database application success is possible only when every affected person enters into absolute, ironclad agreements on each and every relevant data quality issue.

If the data are of very poor quality, it may be impossible to implement one database for all users. Multiple databases may have to be created until all the users agree to cooperate in their data value policies.

Once the data are deemed to be of acceptable quality, the process of data loading specification starts, utilizing all relevant data sources. These sources should be thoroughly analyzed to determine their applicability and coverage of the required database data.

Once all the data sources have been identified, an additional issue must be addressed. If the database's DBMS is static, then data can be loaded only in a certain sequence (owners then members). If the owner data records are not available until after the member data records, then the members must be acquired, set aside, and loaded into the database after the owners are available. In short, the static DBMS database requires database loading to proceed in a definite sequence. If, however, the database's DBMS is dynamic, records can be loaded whenever they are obtained. If there is no owner for a member, then the record merely exists as an orphan until the owner is loaded.

Regardless of whether the DBMS is static or dynamic, an overall schedule for data loading should be created to help establish when database data are to be available for reporting. In addition to the schedule, a data-flow diagram (DFD) type graphic should be created that illustrates the hierarchically organized set of processes necessary to load the database. At the lowest level of this graphic are the primitive record insert operations that transform input data to a stored data record. Taken together, these data transformations become the mini-specifications for the one-time-only data loading subsystem that will be developed in the implementation phase.

Data Transformation Specification

A database data transformation is an interaction of database objects and elements, data integrity rules for the object and element, and the rules that govern the data transformation itself. Data transformations are of two types: updates and reports. Clearly the data transformations whose documentation is most critical are those that affect states within the database, that is, updates. Each and every update data transformation must be documented in the logical database. An example of a data transformation specification is given in Figure 6.8. These update data transformations can then be used as specifications in writing application programs for the data update subsystem.

The data transformations are also a source of semantically correct statements of database actions for natural languages. For example, in Figure 6.9, if there is an education database in which there is an illness record for students, and students are connected via an enrollment record to classes, and classes are one of the records of teachers, is it semantically correct to print all the illnesses related to a particular teacher, especially if some of the illnesses were of a social origin? While the data transformations section of a database specification would not specifically prohibit this operation, it would state the bounds of correct semantic logic for students' illnesses.

The Conceptual Specification Phase

The process of obtaining the name, definition, and rules for each data transformation is analogous to the process of defining the data integrity model. It starts from the database domain, which contains the definitional inferences of the business events that occur within the database system and proceeds through the naming and defining of the various business events until a set of data transformation primitives is reached. A business event is a set of business events that call for data transformations according to a set of rules. Since the phrase "business event" is used within to its own definition, there is the clear implication that a business event is recursive; that is, a business event might well contain other business events.

COMPONENT: DATA TRANSFORMATION

NAME: INSERT CONTRACT

DEFINITION: Insert contract defines the rules that govern the process of creating a new contract with the database.

AFFECTED
OBJECT: CONTRACT

ELEMENTS
AFFECTED: ALL

RULES:
- For a new contract, there must not be an existing contract with the same number.

- No contract can be inserted without a preexisting customer.

- The contract's salesperson must be presently employed.

- The contract-sign-date must not exist in the future.

- The maximum cost must be more than the minimum cost.

- All fields must be valued.

Figure 6.8   Insert Contract Data Transformation

Physical Database Specfication

There is a need to represent business events graphically, and a variation of the data-flow diagramming technique is useful for two reasons. First, each DFD is intended to contain only homogeneous activities; thus, all the business events shown on a DFD represent activities at the same level of specificity.

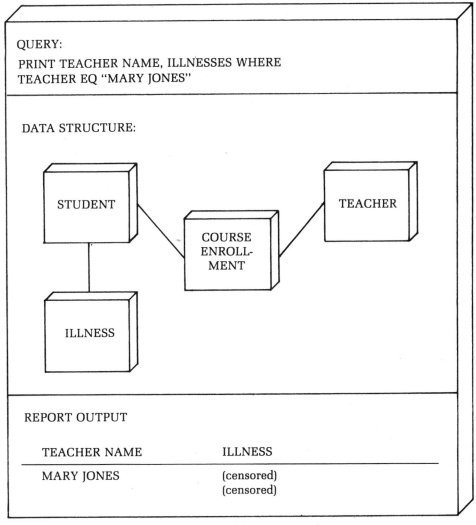

QUERY:

PRINT TEACHER NAME, ILLNESSES WHERE
TEACHER EQ "MARY JONES"

DATA STRUCTURE:

STUDENT

COURSE
ENROLL-
MENT

TEACHER

ILLNESS

REPORT OUTPUT

TEACHER NAME	ILLNESS
MARY JONES	(censored)
	(censored)

Figure 6.9 Limits of Semantic Inferences

Second, a DFD activity might represent a more complex set of activities that are presented on subordinate levels. At the "bottommost" level of the DFD, that is, when a business event contains no subordinate business events, the process represented is the database data transformation. Each transformation is the basis of a minispecification.

Data Update Subsystem Specification

Collections of data transformations become logical components of an overall data update subsystem. An example of the business event, ADD CUSTOMER, is provided in Figure 6.10. During the execution of the business event ADD CUSTOMER, the data transformation rule (Figure 6.8) INSERT CONTRACT must be honored. Also, once the operation is complete, the data integrity rules in Figures 6.4, 6.5, 6.6, and 6.8 must test TRUE. In this example (Figure 6.10), if any INSERT fails, the entire transaction is rolled back (removed).

Physical Database Summary

The physical database within the context of the conceptual specification consists principally of the complete codification of all database update operations. Backing up these operations are the specifications of the data transformations which provide the basis for determining whether the operation is successful. In addition to the specification of the data update subsystem, the data loading subsystem is specified, as well as requirements for backup.

6.5 INTERROGATION SPECIFICATION

Interrogation specification focuses on a general analysis of the complexity of the required or prototypical reports that are to be produced by the database. This general analysis concentrates on understanding the nature of the interrogation task, then on determining the design suitability of the database, and finally on selecting the most appropriate language for access.

Process-Oriented Interrogation

In the first chapter it was clearly stated that the database approach should not be used for process-oriented applications. While that is objectively correct, there are some processes that benefit from database.

An example is the process of computing a paycheck. For a large corporation not using an exception method of computing a paycheck, the database approach can be very helpful. It might provide--in successive steps--all the information necessary to compute a paycheck for a piecework employee.

```
COMPONENT:   BUSINESS EVENT
     NAME:   ADD CUSTOMER


  PSEUDO CODE:

START TRANSACTION

  DO WHILE CUSTOMER EXISTS

    INSERT CUSTOMER, IF FAILURE THEN ROLLBACK

      DO WHILE CONTRACT EXISTS

        INSERT CONTRACT, IF FAILURE THEN ROLLBACK

          DO WHILE ORDER EXISTS

            INSERT ORDER, IF FAILURE THEN ROLLBACK

              DO WHILE ORDER-ITEM EXISTS

                INSERT ORDER-ITEM, IF FAILURE THEN ROLLBACK

              END ORDER-ITEM

          END ORDER

      END CONTRACT

  END CUSTOMER

END TRANSACTION
```

Figure 6.10   Add Customer Business Event

First, the employee identifier would be entered, then the item's identity and the number of items for which the employee is to be compensated. The program would then access a rate record type to compute the gross pay and compute the net pay by accessing all the employees' personnel information. The final paycheck would then be entered in the employees' compensation record type, and the appropriate accrual record types would be updated, including various accounting ledgers.

While the computation of the paycheck is essentially a process, the use of a database could be appropriate, because the information produced is in some sense more important than the paycheck. The information would be retained and used subsequently for research on productivity, profitability, taxes, and the like. Further, the paycheck production process is probably a small part of a very large corporate activity called human resource management. The paycheck production subsystem component of the human resource database is thus a hybrid of an update subsystem and an interrogation subsystem.

If the only application of the database were computing paychecks, the payroll application database design would be oriented toward that use. Record type content would be restricted, and the relationships between records would promote the efficient production of paychecks. If payroll were the only use, the use of a DBMS still might be justified on the basis of these benefits:

o   Concurrent, multiple-user access to data without special precautions.

o   Transaction rollback within programs.

o   Security and privacy of data.

o   Natural language access for ad hoc reports.

o   Automatically implemented data integrity.

o   Programs that are simpler to design, create, understand, and maintain.

Transaction-Oriented Interrogation

A database can also be used as a public library. It is accessed, a piece of information is extracted under a set of conditions, and research is performed. There may be many persons accessing a database in this manner. Since each interrogation has no relationship to a prior one, it should answer each with equal efficiency. This also implies that the organization of the database should be the most natural, rather than be oriented to any of its uses.

Interrogation Tools

As might be expected, multiple languages are available with most DBMSs. Some are oriented to processes; others are oriented to transactions. Regardless of its process or transaction orientation, a DBMS interrogation language is either one that was invented by the DBMS vendor with capabilities suited especially to the DBMS (natural language) or one that consists of a mechanism to interface an ANSI standard compiler language such as COBOL or FORTRAN (a host language interface). DBMS users typically have access to two major compiler language interfaces and three natural languages. A more detailed description of these languages is presented in Chapter 9.

It might seem much simpler to have only one language through which database data could be accessed. While that would seem simpler, it might severely retard the development of natural user-data interactive environments. To many users, the DBMS is the computer. They know no other method of access. So, to them, multiple languages are analogous to the multiple compiler languages available to the programmer, or multiple modes of processing to the systems programmer.

Further, no human programmer is capable of generating an entirely original program in about 15 seconds. That is exactly what the query language does. In one hour of connect time, the ad hoc user can design, program, debug, and execute possibly 20 to 30 original programs. Multiply that by 50 to 100 users, and you have some appreciation of the power of the natural language tool. The big payoff of the database approach comes when many users access a large database without any traditional programmer assistance.

The real value of natural languages is not that they might obviate programmers, but that these languages now free programmers to work on the truly complex jobs that cannot be adequately handled by a natural language.

Database Design Suitability

The object graphic (see Figure 6.7) represents an initial or proposed implementation structure that may be acceptably representative of a significant number of the reports, but not all. In examining all the reports, a general estimate should be made regarding the percentage of records that a particular interrogation touches. This type of analysis is accomplished by examining the report to determine the database record types involved and identifying the approximate record access sequence through the structure. Counts can then be made of the number of database records required to produce the report. The total number of records accessed over a year can be determined by multiplying the report frequency by the number of records touched per report.

If the database is "ideally" designed, each report should touch less than 2 percent of the data to arrive at its answer. If, however, there is a class of reports that consumes significant resources, then possibly this initial or proposed implementation structure that is represented by the object graphic may need to be adjusted. This adjustment could range from adding statistical computation elements such as the TOTAL ORDER COST element depicted in Figure 6.4 to the addition of entirely new--and possibly redundant--types of structures.

For example, if a database is organized to report products sold by a customer over time, then to create a report of sales by product over time requires that the data be processed in an inverse order. If the number of reports that require this product orientation report is such that the entire database system performs unacceptably, then the following alternatives are possible:

o The data must be stored in a completely neutral processing format, as is typical in dynamic DBMSs, which makes all reports less efficient, but possibly acceptable overall.

o The data should be stored in a product orientation and let the customer orientation suffer.

o A redundant data structure that is product oriented should be created. This also means increasing the number of data integrity rules and the domain of the update processing to ensure database integrity and consistency for this new, yet redundant, data structure.

Regrettably, there may be no ideal option, and one may have to choose among these merely tolerable options.

Initial Language Selection

The choice of a specific DBMS interrogation language can affect the amount of effort required to accomplish a given report programming task, the amount of database interaction allowed the language user, and finally the portability of the task itself from one DBMS to the next. Figure 6.11 shows the interaction among these three factors by language type. Again, one may have to choose a tolerable option, rather than an ideal one.

Figure 6.12 provides a cross product of four interrogations, language types, and data models. The analysis assumes--as is generally the case--that all types of DBMS can perform any of the interrogations in host language interface (HLI); that neither the network nor the hierarchical data model DBMSs have a procedure oriented language (POL); that most ILF and relational systems do not have query-update and report-writer languages separate from POLs; and that all interrogations require data from several data elements in each record type.

Language Selection Criteria	INTERROGATION LANGUAGE TYPE			
	HLI	POL	RW	QUL
Task Development Effort	High	Med.	Med.	Low
Relative Work Units	100	10	10	1
Level of User Control over Database Interaction	Low	Med.	Med.	High
Range of Portability from one DBMS to Another of the Same Data Model	Med. to High	Low	Low	Low

HLI = Host Language Interface   RW = Report Writer
POL = Procedure-Oriented Language   QUL = Query-Update Language

Figure 6.11   Interrogation Language Selection Criteria

Since the effort required to create a host language interface (HLI) program is significantly greater than that required for a natural language program, it is important to know whether the organization employs a sufficient number of skilled personnel to implement the HLI aspects of an application. All indicators might point to requiring an HLI, but if the implementation requires more staff effort than is available, another database design and even another DBMS might have to be employed to permit the development of most interrogation through natural language programs, even though the DBMS might fulfill the requirements of the database application less effectively.

Interrogation Summary

Two issues enter into the analysis of interrogation. The first, database design suitability, requires that an assessment be made of the practicality of the design and a decision made as to whether the database design should be modified to achieve economical operation. Second, the available interrogation languages must be assessed with respect to the complexity of the interrogation requirements, so that estimates can be developed for design, programming, and operations.

DATA MODEL AND NATURAL LANGUAGE TYPE	INTERROGATION INVOLVING			
	PRODUCT, PRODUCT-SPECIFI-CATION	REGION, SALESPERSON, CUSTOMER	PRODUCT-PRICE, ORDER-ITEM	PRODUCT, ORDER, ORDER-ITEM, SALESPERSON
Network (Fig. 2.3) QUL/RW	Yes	Yes	Yes	Yes
Hierarchical (Fig. 2.4) QUL/RW	Yes	No	No	No
ILF (Fig. 2.5) POL	Yes	Yes	Yes	Yes
Relational (Fig. 2.6) POL	Yes	Yes	Yes	Yes

Figure 6.12   Interrogation Language Selection

6.6   SYSTEM CONTROL

A database prototype is very useful in obtaining critical information about the various components of system control. When the prototype is being demonstrated, users can be questioned about what kind of information is needed for audit trails, backup and recovery, and the like. The information should be in the form of requirements that must be met to satisfy legal, privacy and security needs.

Five components of system control are dramatically affected by the static or dynamic nature of the DBMS: audit trails, backup and recovery, reorganization, multiple database processing, and concurrent operations. There must be a very good understanding of the critical need characteristics in each of these areas.

For example, if a static DBMS required a complete reloading of the database every time an element characteristic was changed, and if that happened seven days a week and twice on Sunday, the static DBMS would never allow the application to get off the ground. On the other hand, such changes would be practical with a dynamic DBMS, because the effect of the changes would be restricted to a particular record type rather than to the entire database.

6.7 DATABASE SYSTEM VALIDATION

A database system consists of its at-rest (data integrity model) and in-motion (data transformation model) parts, which must be examined in combination to validate the complete database system specification.

The data integrity model is used to validate the scope and comprehensiveness of the data transformation model. The components of the data integrity model should be functionally exhausted at the same time that the review of the data transformation model is completed.

The converse should also be true. This means that there should be no more, and no fewer, business events than are required to satisfy the requirements of the data integrity model. And there should be no more, and no fewer, data integrity model components than are loaded, updated, and reported with business events.

In short, if the design is ideal, the two models will balance; furthermore, they both should satisfy the requirements set forth in the database domain.

The two models can be unbalanced in three ways. First, if the data integrity model is a superset, the transformation model must be underspecified. The data integrity may have been too "blue sky," or there may not have been an adequate search for relevant business events.

Second, if the data transformation is a superset of the data integrity model, the data integrity model is probably underspecified and should be enlarged.

Third, the models will be unbalanced when the functional capabilities are neither of the above, but are intersecting. In the case where the two models are intersecting the remedies applied to the prior two cases are required.

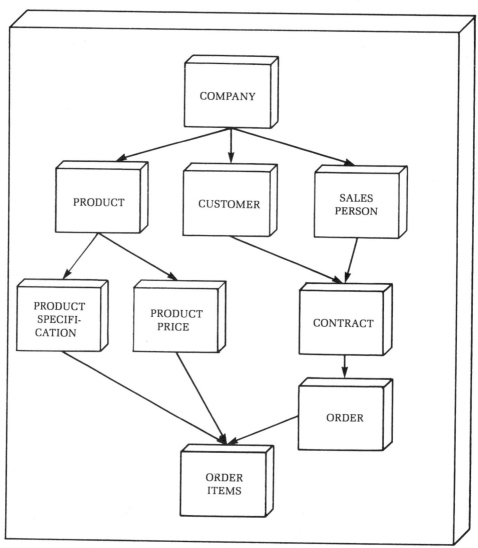

Figure 6.13   Sales and Marketing Object Graphic

Once the specification is validated, a prototype of the database system should be created and then rigorously evaluated. This is best done through a dynamic DBMS. Initially, a prototype is constructed of the entire database system. It is then demonstrated to significant users. Their suggestions are incorporated whenever possible, and a new prototype is then created.

This iterative design validation process is continued until the design has become stable. At each iteration, the documentation of all relevant specifications is adjusted. At the end, a final specification document is created. This single document represents both the logical and physical database components of the conceptual specification of the database project. The prototype is also useful in validating the interrogation and system control aspects of the conceptual specification.

6.8 HUMAN SUPPORT SUBSYSTEMS

Once the conceptual specification is complete, an effort should be made to optimize the activities people in the organization perform, so they can use the specified database system more effectively. To accomplish this optimization, an understanding must be developed of the human or manual activities being performed within the old environment, so that during the implementation of the new environment the required changes in activities that have been identified and quantified can be introduced.

The techniques used to identify required changes are similar to those typically employed in structured analysis. This process defines--in sequence--the environment's "old physical," then its "current logical," then its "new logical," and, finally, its "new physical." The database approach, in contrast, defines the "new logical" at the outset during the conceptual specification phase. Then, with this "target" clearly in sight, the "old physical" that must change is transformed to its "new physical" form.

As an example, if under the old system salespersons reported directly to the company (see Figure 6.13), then the old way of handling sales reports would certainly have to change, since there are now regions. Salespersons should file their reports with their regional offices rather than send them to company headquarters. If none of the old procedures are changed, the regions will be without sales reports, as the salespersons will still be sending their reports to the central office. The old physical data flow diagram (DFD) would show that the old way does not fit the new database, and that transformation to a new physical process will have to be undertaken. That is, salespersons will send their reports to regional offices which, in turn, will send statistics to company headquarters.

The new way may produce side effects--delays in delivering statistics to the company level, for example. If this is unacceptable, the sales reports may have to be entered directly by the salespersons and a computer report made available immediately to the regional manager. Once approved, the regional manager could signal the database system that the region's data were available for inclusion in company statistics.

Only when all the human support subsystems have been identified and researched for impact can the full effect of a database be determined. Without the support of the organizations that use the database, the project is sure to fail.

6.9 CONCEPTUAL SPECIFICATION SUMMARY

Developing a conceptual specification is similar to building a model. It is the same as the real thing in every aspect except size. Thus, there is a natural tendency to simply promote the prototype to adult status and "let'r rip." That has often been done in the past, and that is exactly what happened: the prototype disintegrated under the load. There were little bits of integrity all over the place. A design strategy that is appropriate for a prototype may not be at all appropriate for the fully implemented system.

The purpose of a prototype of a database application is to maximize the capability to change the design and minimize the effort necessary to make the design changes. And when that is possible, high performance is not possible with today's technology.

In contrast, the purpose of implementing the real database system is to maximize efficiency of production by prebiasing--if necessary--the order and the structure of the records in such a way as to accomplish this goal. When that happens, the most likely result is severely degraded design flexibility, as well as a degraded capability to handle all interrogations with equal efficiency. But that is quite acceptable when the database is sufficiently well designed to make radical change unneccessary.

The conceptual specification is really, then, a process through which a complete prototype of the database application can be built, demonstrated, and validated prior to implementation.

Review Questions

In traditionally designed systems, the database design can only be validated after the system is implemented. At that point, about 85% of all monies are spent. Developing the conceptual specification of the database project as has been described should expend no more than 25% of the project's resources. That's about three times less money, and considerably sooner in the project's life-cycle. Further, if significant changes are needed, the cost for change in the traditionally designed system could easily be another 50% of the project's resources. Using the design process described in this chapter, the cost would probably be only about 5 to 10%.

6.10 REVIEW QUESTIONS

1. List and describe seven major steps of logical database specification.

2. Compare and contrast the different types of graphic specification utilized in the conceptual specification.

3. What are the components of element specification? What part do elements play in the conceptual specification phase?

4. Describe the role of the E-R diagram.

5. What must be done to data elements before assigning them to objects?

6. How are the contents of Figures 6.4 through 6.6 and Figure 6.8 interrelated? How does each contribute to the development of a complete database specification?

7. What occurs during model validation?

8. What are the four most important benefits of the design process?

9. During which phase are the size and number of databases determined? Upon what criteria is this decision based?

The Conceptual Specification Phase

10. What is accomplished during interrogation specification?

11. Why is system control greatly affected by the type of database?

12. Explain why attention must be paid to the human support subsystems of a database project.

13. Give a general definition of the conceptual specification phase.

7 Implementation Phase

7.1 ACTIVITIES AND SCOPE

The implementation phase of a database project is the set of activities that bind the conceptual specification to a particular DBMS and to a particular mode of operation. Thus, it includes activities in all four database components.

Logical database activities consist of a final review of the conceptual specification and then transformation into a particular DBMS that includes the creation of both a schema and various subschemata.

Physical database activities are quite intense. The storage structure size is determined and the database's access strategy is selected. The data loading subsystem is completely written, debugged, documented, and thoroughly tested. The data necessary for the first big load is prepared. The final activity, data update, is carefully planned. A complete subsystem is created to ensure absolute control over any changes in the database.

Interrogation activities are directed toward creation of the reporting subsystems. They should be performed in this phase only if they are found to be prerequisites for database system operation. The implementation of unessential reporting subsystems will only cause delays; therefore, only those reporting subsystems that are deemed absolutely essential should be implemented.

All the software and procedures needed to support the database's system control component are fully implemented, documented, and tested during this phase.

Implementation Phase

Many modern DBMSs offer very attractive opportunities to accelerate the delivery of tested code. For example, through the effective use of natural languages for updating and reporting, a problem that took four to six months to design, code, test, and document in a compiler language such as COBOL could well be accomplished in less than one week.

Accelerated development is possible for two reasons. First, a sophisticated natural language significantly reduces the actual number of lines of code needed to accomplish a data updating or reporting function, which in turn reduces coding and testing time. Second, because the natural language program is often self-evident in its purpose and logic, the amount of time traditionally spent on design, testing, and documentation is so drastically reduced as to be almost nonexistent.

Clearly then, before any estimates can be made of the amount of time required to implement the database project's conceptual specification, there must be a very good understanding of the productivity improvement that can be derived from sophisticated natural languages.

In addition to these technology-oriented products, the following supports are also created or installed: hotline (for both the application and the DBMS), standards, test data, documentation, and training. At the end of all these activities, there is a final overall test period. If the tests are successful, the database application is declared operational.

7.2 LOGICAL DATABASE

The data integrity model, defined in the conceptual specification phase, is now transformed to conform to the requirements of a particular DBMS. After this is done, the schema can be created. What is important about the schema is not only that it contains the semantics of a database, but that the logical design is derived from a complete data integrity model of the database specification. The schema is, then, a mechanism for translating the functional user's logical database into the DBMS's logical database.

Complete specifications for each active subschema must also be contained in the logical database section of the application documentation. In a way that parallels the schema's functioning as a translation mechanism, the subschema serves as a mechanism for translating from the DBMS's logical database to the various host and natural languages.

102

Logical Database

Static Data Model Choices

The two data models within the static classification are network and hierarchical. The choices then, assuming an IBM computing environment, are Cullinet's IDMS or CINCOM's TOTAL for the network and IBM's IMS or INTEL's SYSTEM 2000 for the hierarchy.

In very general terms, IDMS has a far richer record structure and relationship capability than does TOTAL for the network data model. For example, IDMS allows multiple member sets, singular sets, version linguistics subtleties, and a significant number of physical performance tools that facilitate the design and implementation of large, very sophisticated databases.

For hierarchical models the choice is also restricted to just two DBMSs, IMS and SYSTEM 2000. IMS can be more finely tuned for very large applications than SYSTEM 2000. The price paid for that tuning capability is a significantly larger manpower requirement for almost every DBMS activity than that of SYSTEM 2000. The price paid for SYSTEM 2000's simplicity is a lesser capacity to handle the truly large application. Over a billion characters is considered large.

Another big difference between SYSTEM 2000 and IMS is that IMS's storage structure and access strategy are designed only for standard reporting, whereas SYSTEM 2000's storage structure and access strategy can be tuned almost as well as IMS's for standard reporting and can also be tuned to handle the sophisticated interactive query. To accomplish interactive or heuristic queries, IMS offers DB2, IBM's newest relational DBMS entry, which requires a data extract prior to any query session.

If the application is of moderate size (say, less than a billion characters), if manpower is not in plentiful supply, and if there is a need to make ad hoc interrogations through a query language, then SYSTEM 2000's ease of use makes it a better choice than IMS.

If, on the other hand, the application is quite large and you can throw a lot of resources into it, and if there is only a need for standard reporting, then IMS is a better choice because it and the database can be tuned to the needs of the application.

The critical difference between the network and hierarchical data model DBMSs is that the network data model can explicitly define complex data structures, while the hierarchical data model cannot. Both hierarchical DBMSs can, however, indirectly accomplish these network structures, but not in any straightforward manner. If they could, then they would be network data model DBMSs.

Dynamic Data Model Choices

The two dynamic data models are independent logical file (ILF) and relational. There are many DBMSs in the ILF category but only a few in the relational category.

Only one ILF, ADABAS, seems to be capable of performing large production jobs. It is not likely, however, that ADABAS could outperform IMS, IDMS, or SYSTEM 2000 in a very large, complex production job. It was just not built to do that kind of work. The other remaining ILF systems are oriented to the decision support or MIS-oriented application of small to moderate size with five to ten record types. These DBMSs are rich in statistics, graphics, and other manager-oriented facilities.

One ILF, FOCUS, has taken an interesting and different approach in marketing. FOCUS can reside alongside IMS, IDMS, or TOTAL in user installations and interface with their databases to provide an interactive ad hoc reporting environment. FOCUS can also construct its own databases and support them with the normal set of DBMS facilities.

While there are relational systems on the market, generally their capabilities cannot approach those of the ILF DBMSs. Choosing a relational DBMS over a well-appointed ILF might be difficult to justify.

Design Modifications

Once the DBMS has been selected, the type of design modifications that must be made to adapt correctly and efficiently the data integrity model to the capabilities provided by the DBMS can be determined. These modifications are of two types: efficiency considerations and integrity.

Efficiency Considerations.   Efficiency considerations include the establishment of redundant data in multiple record types to avoid processing formal interrecord relationships. For example, in Figure 2.3, if the name of the current salesperson is placed in the contract record type, then the salesperson's record type does not have to be accessed to find the person's name. On the other hand, if the salesperson's name is in the contract record, there is the additional burden of updating that element in every affected contract each time the salesperson changes. That becomes a problem only when the update has been forgotten several times, producing a database with questionable integrity.

It is safe to include redundant data only when it is historical. For example, in the case of the initial salesperson's name, integrity would be upset only if the name were wrong, and that is not the problem of database.

Derived data is another type of redundancy. For example, in a census database there might be computed statistics at the national level, the state level, and the local community level, and then the raw data. To recompute these statistics every time the corresponding raw data were retrieved would consume too much computer time. On the other hand, if the raw data were updated, these derived statistics would also have to be updated.

Other types of efficiency considerations relate to the allocation of the database's record types to storage structures. Each DBMS has different storage structure characteristics, so each has to be examined to determine the optimal number of record types per database. The goal is to minimize computer processing for all the DBMS operations while at the same time minimizing the number of relationships between databases.

If there is a high concentration of record types in one physical database and there is also a need to add element types, most DBMSs require that the database be brought off-line and reorganized. By reducing the number of record types in the database, less of the database has to be brought off-line. But this reduced cost in reorganization produces a fractured physical structure that consumes extra computer resources to generate complex production reports.

There are many other efficiency considerations, such as fixed or variable length records and elements, generalized or specialized element types, and the like. Each of these must be considered in order to determine the most appropriate alternative for computer implementation.

It should be obvious that the database approach can become very complex and technical. It should also be clear that none of these topics has anything to do with the inherent logical design of a database. These considerations deal only with the implementation of an already designed database. That is exactly why the two activities must be kept apart. If they are not, the functional people will throw up their hands and walk out. And that will leave us right where we are now: knee-deep is a gross technical quagmire. The American Heritage Dictionary (1978) defines a quagmire as "a difficult or precarious situation from which extraction is almost impossible." Doesn't it seem as if the word was invented just for data processing?

Integrity Considerations. It is of little consequence that an application runs fast or slow if it is incorrect. Having database integrity means that under all situations and for all users, the same question produces the same answer and has the same meaning.

Disintegration very often begins when the database's design is being transformed from its generalized form to that required by the DBMS. If an element from one record type is redundantly included in another record type without clearly specifying all the necessary interrecord type update rules, it is likely that neither the schema nor the programs that update the data will contain the remaining rules or clear up ambiguous specifications. In short, an incomplete or ambiguous specification will very likely produce an incomplete or ambiguous implementation.

Suppose, for example, that the salesperson's name has been placed in the contract record, and one update clerk thought it was for the initial salesperson and another thought it was for the current salesperson. Confusion would surely ensue when commission checks were issued for current sales, or when bonuses were paid on the basis of initiating accounts.

Disintegration can be due to an incomplete specification or to an improper transformation. In either case, the process of resolution must be the same. Work must stop, and the problem must be referred to the functional users for resolution. When they have resolved it and the data integrity model component of the conceptual specification has been updated, work can recommence.

7.3 THE PHYSICAL DATABASE

The activities involved in development of the application's physical database include definition of the database's storage structure, selection of the most appropriate database access strategy, creation of the data loading subsystem, and creation of the data update subsystem.

The data transformation model that contains descriptions of all the business events becomes the data update subsystem. Also included in this subsystem are all the data integrity rules that the chosen DBMS does not allow to be coded into or invoked from the schema.

The Physical Database

Storage Structure

The storage structure of an implemented database is the set of physical files that contain the data. Since each DBMS has a different type of storage structure, the organization of the DBMS's generated database should be analyzed to determine the optimal configuration for all database data. Generally the dynamic DBMS places each record type into a separate physical file, while the static DBMS allows multiple record types to be in one physical file.

Statistics should be developed about the size and organization of each of the DBMS's physical files to help determine why certain processes in the implemented database perform at less than a desired throughput rate. To perform such analyses, database statistics such as size and DBMS file structure, application statistics such as frequency and extent of updates, and information about interrogation modules and their complexity all contribute to an understanding.

The process of determining the appropriate database storage structure is iterative. That is, a file organization hypothesis is created, the relevant record types are assigned, and then a performance analysis of typical updates and retrievals is conducted. If these typical processes are not accomplished in an acceptable manner, an adjustment is made. Then the performance analysis begins again. It is doubtful whether there ever can be an absolutely ideal storage structure. Often the best achievement is a compromise among data redundancy, update efficiency, report performance, and integrity.

The design of the storage structure is typically communicated to the DBMS by a data storage definition language (DSDL). The DSDL is a translation mechanism operating between the DBMS's schema and the computer's operating system (O/S). The DSDL communicates to the O/S the desired physical file organization that is to contain the database's dictionary, indexes, relationships, and data.

Access Strategy

The access strategy of an implemented database consists of the mechanisms for record selection, retrieval, insertion, and deletion that are built into the database by the DBMS. These mechanisms--indexes and relationship pointers--are employed by the DBMS to accomplish database access. The quantity of each must be chosen carefully to achieve the optimal balance between update and retrieval.

Implementation Phase

As might be expected, every DBMS has a different access strategy. Some DBMSs do not have indexes, except for the primary key. If the application requires only random access of single records then the access strategy can be set up quickly and easily. However, if particular sets of records need to be found, intricate gyrations may have to be established.

For example, to select records of a certain class, say all A#1 salespersons, the DBMS might scan the record type's file to find a particular class of records, or access a specific record type whose sole purpose is to represent classes of records. That is, there is a record occurrence that represents A#1 salespersons. By accessing the class record type through the primary key value of "A#1," all of that record's member records, that is, salesperson's records, would be the A#1 salespersons.

Relationships. A relationship is analogous to an index in that it links records according to a certain criterion. Some DBMSs allow records to be related through relationships (information-bearing) that are not based on any linking value. An example of an information-bearing relationship is children related to an employee without any of the parent's identifying information (such as PARENT-ID) stored in the dependent's record. An example of a value-based relationship is the assignment of an employee to a particular department, with the department's name included in the employee's record.

As can be seen in Figure 2.3, there are, in general, these types of relationships:

o   Owner-to-member relationship, as in CUSTOMER to CONTRACT.

o   Member-to-owner relationship, as in CONTRACT to CUSTOMER or SALESPERSON.

o   Member-to-member, as in one ORDER to another for a given CONTRACT.

o   Member-to-member for members of different types, as in ACTIVE-CONTRACTS, INACTIVE-CONTRACTS, or TERMINATED-CONTRACT. (Note: unlike the situation presented in Figure 2.3, each variation of the CONTRACT record type would be separately defined.)

o   Owner-to-members of different types, as in a CUSTOMER having any of the three different CONTRACTS.

These five are some of the more obvious relationships among the CUSTOMER, SALESPERSON, and CONTRACT record types. There are many more, and the decision as to whether some, all, or none of them should be implemented requires balancing the overall cost of retrieval without the facility against the cost of its maintenance.

For example, if 20 of the 100 salespersons in a given region are A#1, then locating these employees could involve accessing--on average--40 records that do not contain the A#1 criteria. If an index or relationship existed, the 40 wasted record accesses would be saved.

If the A#1 salesperson classification is made monthly, and if 10 salespersons come into and out of the A#1 category, then 10 salespersons will not change and 10 will have the category added. The total number of record accesses to make the change will be 60 (3 accesses per record). If the report is run only once per month, the relative cost, 60 maintenance accesses plus 20 record accesses versus the sequential search of 60 accesses clearly indicates that the facility is not cost-effective from the computer point of view. Other factors may, however, tip the scale in the other direction. For example, with the facility it may be possible to use a natural language.

The DBMS employs the various types of relationships and indexes to select, retrieve, store, and delete records. Knowledge of the efficiencies of these capabilities is essential in order to determine the appropriate number of indexes that access records within a single record type, and the appropriate relationships that enable traversal between record types.

Indexes. Indexes permit faster access of data records, either singly or by groups of records that are of the same type. For example, there might be an index on the EMPLOYEE-ID. Upon reference, the employee's record would be selected and returned to the application program faster than if the file were accessed sequentially or serially.

If the employee's educational degree element were indexed and if the selection criterion were DEGREE = MS, then all the employees with an MS degree would be retrieved in a group and, depending on the DBMS, presented to the run-unit in a specific sequence.

Indexes and relationships interact. For example, if an employee's DEGREE was in a repeating group, then the index would find the instances of MS, but only the relationships would traverse back to the employee who is the "owner" of the MS degree.

Access Strategy Trade-offs. The positive aspects of indexes and relationships have already been described. These facilities also have a negative impact, in that they too must be updated when records are added, deleted, or modified. For example, if a teacher record is added to the database, the value of the teacher's degree element must be properly incorporated into the set of index facilities to permit the record to be found quickly. Further, the record must be incorporated into the various teaching assignment relationships.

A proper balance must be achieved between the resources expended for update and those expended for retrieval. Extra features such as indexes and relationships do optimize retrievals, but they also increase the cost of updating. If the database has a high volume of updates as compared to retrievals, then the environment will run faster if there are fewer indexes and relationships to update along with the addition, deletion, and modification of records. The converse is equally true.

Simply, the facts are that the access time for a record is inversely proportional to the number of indexes and relationships, while the update time is in direct proportion. That means that these two access-enhancement facilities must be used wisely and sparingly.

In summary, great care should be exercised when using a DBMS that is rich in index and relationship facilities so that when an application implementation is complete, you have not caused the conceptual specification to be implemented in a functionally unresponsive manner.

Data Loading Subsystem

A major portion of the initial database activity involves data loading. The data loading subsystem, specified in the conceptual specification phase, must now be designed, coded, and thoroughly tested. The testing must be thorough, because once a database is loaded with flawed data, they are almost impossible to find and clean-up. As a result, the only safe course is to clean up the data right from the start, and then begin the data loading process.

The Physical Database

Once the data loading system is created, tested, documented, and made ready, the actual process of constructing the source data files for data loading preparation can begin. Actually, analysis and correction of source data should begin long before this. There is a great tendency to load and go, and if the database does not self-destruct, then all must be correct.

Data analysis should not stop with its loading into a database. It can stop when all the loaded data are certified as correct and conforming to the current set of data policies. Because validation of historical data is such a big task, and because some of the prior policies under which the historical data were collected cannot be determined, some projects start only with new data.

Data Update Subsystem

Once a database is loaded, it is thereafter maintained through a formally declared and established data update subsystem. Because every update has the potential to harm the integrity of the database, it is critically important to have all data update policies and procedures centrally designed and administered.

Each data update module is a computerized version of a data transformation that was specified in the conceptual specification phase. A logical collection of related data transformations is a business event. Whether the implemented business event is a single host language interface (HLI) program with a series of data transformation paragraphs or a collection of small on-line transactions that are connected together by some type of job control language is not terribly important. What is important is that each and every data transformation rule be properly executed, so that after the update transaction is completed, all the data integrity rules test true.

Traditional methods of module design, testing, implementation and maintenance can be used to build the data update subsystem. In addition to traditional system documentation, the database environment that surrounds each update transaction must also be specified. The database environment includes a description of the locks imposed by the DBMS software on the database, the quantity of resources that will be consumed per update, the daily volumes for the transaction, an estimate of the degradation effects the transaction is likely to have on the organization of the storage structure, and what methods exist to back out the effects of the transaction once it has executed against the database.

Database Maintenance

Maintaining the database as a single entity is critically important. There must be a clearly defined and documented procedure to carry out the backing-up and restoration of the database. The number of backups and the ability to recreate current database versions depend on the reliability of both the DBMS and the computer system and on the quality of the data update subsystem. It depends on the data update subsystem because if legal but incorrect updates occur over a long period of time--before discovery--then they must be backed out, and all the transactions that were made on the basis of these incorrect values must be rerun.

Physical Database Summary

The documentation surrounding the implementation of the physical database is very important. It describes exactly how the database was loaded, and how it is updated, maintained, backed-up, and recovered. Initially, the most critical component of the physical database is the entire process of data loading. Thereafter, the most critical aspect is the centrally designed and administered data update subsystem.

7.4   INTERROGATION

Interrogation, or the creation of one or more major reporting subsystems, cannot be on the critical path of the database project. It is, rather, an activity that can be performed by the functional users whenever they are so inclined. The same cannot be said about conceptual specification of data integrity, data transformations, data loading, data update, and the various system control components. These must all be done first, correctly, before the database project can be declared operational. Spending time on interrogation modules to the exclusion of data loading, update, or system control is tantamount to pursuing database suicide.

7.5   SYSTEM CONTROL

Eight of the nine system control areas are addressed during implementation. Each may be composed of DBMS utilities, natural language commands, user-written programs, or possibly combinations of all of these. Although system control components interact, as described in the system control summary of Chapter 9, it is best to treat all but concurrent operations and multiple database processing as separately defined, implemented, operated, and maintained subsystems.

Audit Trails

The audit trail's content method of capture, storage, and utilization for reports or possibly for database restoration, as defined in the conceptual specification, must now be clearly implemented. A set of prototype modules that uses the audit trail facility should be created and thoroughly tested to validate its design before the actual facilities are finally set in place.

Once implemented, the whole facility needs to be documented in much the same way as the most critical data update transaction. While a bit recursive, special attention must be paid to the system control aspects of audit trails, including the audit trail of the audit trail, its backup and recovery, the database lockout that exists while the audit trail is written, and the like.

Backup and Recovery

This topic, which has been partially treated under database maintenance, must receive considerable attention, as it may be the only way to fix a database subsequent to its damage.

The database approach itself has created the need for elaborate backup and recovery. In traditional systems, many files were created from others, and when one got destroyed the extract programs could always be run again. Not so in database, for if the ideal is reached, there is only one storage place for each fact.

Well-defined procedures must exist for taking backups and for accomplishing recovery under any and all unforeseen circumstances, as those are the only circumstances in effect when a database is in desperate need of recovery.

Careful estimates must be made of the resources required to backup and recover a database at various times during the month. The various data maintenance cycles can dramatically affect database size, efficient database organization, and the size of the recovery log file--and all these factors affect the time required for recovery. With this information, a proper choice can be made of any periodic backup cycles that would permit the recovery log to be refreshed and thus shorten the time required for database recovery.

Implementation Phase

Message Processing

Users are besieged with messages. They come from many different places in a database environment. Among the sources are the operating system, the DBMS, and the application. The database application and the DBMS must have a centralized scheme for all messages that surface to users.

A central directory of messages should be built so that when new ones are added, or old ones are modified, the messages file can be centrally updated and reprinted. Ideally, the DBMS should allow for message definition and, as required, automatic message logging. Logging of the user identification of messages is especially useful for identifying those in need of training.

Reorganization

Databases need periodic reorganization. This is especially true of static ones. They often are designed to have certain data records placed very near others, so that certain production reports can be processed more rapidly than others. As updating progresses, the initial placement of records cannot be maintained, and that results in database disorganization.

In Figure 2.4, if the DBMS allowed ORDER-ITEM records to be stored "near" their ORDER records (that is, within the same physical database record), but over time the space set aside for those ORDER-ITEM records for specific orders was exhausted, the new ORDER-ITEM records would be stored somewhere else (in a different physical record) in the database. Retrieval of these new records would take longer, as they are not proximate to their ORDER record. Reorganization can remedy this situation by reloading the ORDER and ORDER-ITEM records, after having first set aside room for all the records that comprise a complete customer order.

In addition to data disorganization, other supporting storage structure components, such as indexes, may also become disorganized. Their reorganization can often have a dramatic effect on database performance, in terms of both computer efficiency and user-perceived speed of interactive operation.

Benchmark tests need to be created to measure certain critical database performances. These tests can be run at specific intervals to develop statistics on database performance. These statistics indicate the need for database reorganization before serious performance degradation occurs.

Multiple Database Processing.

Figures 2.4 through 2.6, in conjunction with Figures 6.11 and 6.12, illustrate the need for multiple database processing. If a hierarchical DBMS is being employed and a user needs a report showing the average order value by salesman by region, then the DBMS must possess some mechanism to bridge the dynamic relationship between SALESPERSON and CONTRACT.

Some DBMSs allow multiple database processing, while others do not. When using a DBMS in the latter category, ways need to be invented to get around that restriction. Once found, procedures ensuring proper lockouts during any multiple database update processing need to be established. These procedures should be available to any programmer who needs to carry out operations affecting multiple databases.

Concurrent Operations

When two or more users retrieve the same CONTRACT (see Figure 2.4) record, review the data, and then post changes, the record finally stored is sure to displease all but one of the users. To complicate the situation further, if the various users also add order records, the elements contained in the CONTRACT record's elements (see Figure 6.4) will certainly contain interesting numbers.

Since neither of these results is desired, certain operations must have exclusive access to the record. Exclusive use is achieved through locking. Some locks enable the user to retrieve and hold a record until it is updated; other locks permit multiple record types to be locked. Finally, some can lock the entire database. The specified database must be examined to determine the exact requirements for locking, and these locks must be set in place and thoroughly tested to ensure that there are no undesired side effects.

Some DBMS operations are not allowed to take place while others are executing--retrieval and database reorganization, for example. These special operations actually lock others out of the ability to execute. Such operations should be identified, verified, and carefully documented. This will help prevent a user from initiating an operation that locks a database at the wrong time.

Finally, some operations effectively lock others out, and therefore must be precluded during prime time. Suppose, for example, that the database in Figure 2.3 experienced batch order update runs of 20,000 new orders each day. If the update run is executed in the middle of the afternoon, it is likely that interactive queries will slow considerably. To preclude this slow-down, certain types of update operations should be run only in non-prime time. In short, the application must be analyzed to identify determine these potential performance bottlenecks and to establish mechanisms to avoid them.

Security and Privacy

The main protection of a database is achieved through effective use of subschemata, program restrictions, and the like. In addition to these, a sophisticated DBMS offers capabilities for data value screening and for element utilization in the read, selection, and update clauses.

Once the data update subsystem and interrogation sub-systems are in place, the numbers and types of users can be known. As a result, the necessary procedures can be established to effectively create and maintain whatever subschemata and other security mechanisms are necessary.

Database files may also be accessed from operating system utilities. Protection from such utilities may have to be established--for example, by having database files specially tagged and the DBMS modified so that operating system utilities will not honor requests to act against these specially marked files.

Special DBMS Version Configuration

Sometimes a database is required to handle very different updating and reporting demands at the same time. For example, during prime time, a database might be required to efficiently handle on-line, interactive queries, and capture data and update the database immediately. At night, the system might be required to handle very large batch update runs, or process large volumes of data to produce reports. Because of these very different performance demands, there is normally great latitude in the configuration of DBMS executable code (load) modules that are used by the application modules that capture user updates and handle report requests.

For example, the number and sizes of buffer pools may be established and changed; the DBMS subroutines may or may not be included in various configurations; and finally, the number of overlays of DBMS routines can be changed and reorganized to either expand or contract the amount of computer memory the DBMS consumes. All of these factors, taken together, can necessitate the creation of 5 to 15 different versions of a DBMS. To handle such a number, each different version must be carefully documented so that it is used effectively.

System Control Summary

System control consists of a set of activities unique to database. They all must be very well understood and managed. While each different DBMS has different implementations of these capabilities, each has them all in one format or another. Knowledge and documentation of each capability enable effective and safe database use.

7.6 IMPLEMENTATION SUPPORTS

The five database environment supports--hotline, standards, test data, documentation, and training--are more than just supports; they are absolutely required foundations. Each must be implemented with great care and then updated and maintained throughout the life of the project.

Hotline

There are many different reasons for having hotlines. Normally they are restricted to systems software, such as operating systems. Seldom are they set up for applications. However, a database application is systems software to its users, because it is a generalized set of computer programs through which users accomplish database application activities. That is the same relationship that a programmer has with the language used to create a program.

In addition to the application hotline, which may be only one person, there should be one or more hotline persons for a DBMS. This group should serve the needs of both host language users and natural language users. Additionally, they should be very knowledgeable about the internals of the DBMS so that it can be properly utilized.

Another duty of the hotline is to identify, isolate, and follow through DBMS bugs with the DBMS vendor to ensure that the DBMS is as error-free as possible. When a bug has been isolated and absolutely known to produce bad results, the bug needs to be formed into a testing module and then added to the testing library for the next DBMS release. This complete set of DBMS testing modules should be run each time a new version of the DBMS is installed to validate that old bugs have been fixed, to identify the ones not fixed, and possibly to discover new ones.

The hotline groups should hold regularly scheduled seminars or workshops for application designers and users to pass on any new or updated information. Finally, the hotline groups should publish a newsletter for all users of the database. This would contain helpful hints on enhancing the effectiveness of application or database usage, as well as information on newly discovered bugs and ways to work around them.

Standards

Standards are a formal codification of the procedures and guidelines by which work is structured and performed. In the database approach, standards are especially important. This is because the goal of the approach is to make the whole system public. The public must therefore have confidence that everyone is going to see the system the same way and that data are presented to the system according to the same rules and regulations.

Therefore, standards must exist for every aspect of the database project. There must be one for every component of the logical database, the physical database, and system control. There need not be as strict a set of standards for interrogation, since reporting subsystems do not change values.

The following major benefits can be derived from the implementation of and adherence to a good set of standards.

o   The stifling of innovation. Stifling innovation is the only way to get a large system out within budget and on time. Innovation belongs in the laboratory, not on the production line.

o   The promotion of work exchange. In a database project there are so many players that work exchange--without detailed explanations--is vitally necessary.

o   The production of cleaner code, which in turn requires less debugging.

Test Data

Test data should be so real that they reflect every imaginable prejudice typically found in the live database. The many uses of test data include prototyping, training, DBMS bug detection, and demonstrations. The best use is in the creation of a prototype.

Implementation Supports

Users are actually enticed into participating in the demonstration by having provocative interactions with realistic data.

Test data should be designed to ensure meaningful evaluations of almost every aspect of the DBMS. The data should be such that when the results are produced there is no doubt about whether the processor is working correctly. In a database environment, some of the test data should be in standard access file form for testing data loading and data update, and the data should contain both good and bad data to test every case. There should also be a test database that can be used to validate interrogation programs, data update programs, and the various capabilities within system control.

One of the most critical uses of test data is in detecting DBMS bugs. If at all possible, the test database should also be available to the DBMS vendor. If a user reports a bug, and if it can be duplicated on the test database, then it is almost certainly a DBMS software bug. Further, if the vendor has the same test database, the bug can be replicated immediately.

Realistic test data can be used to enhance the quality of training. They can then be used in the various training courses to teach application concepts, DBMS concepts, and workshops that examine the ramifications of data trends.

A final use of test. data is to predict resource consumptions. Test cases should be constructed that test certain aspects of the DBMS's storage structure and access strategy. Knowing that certain types of updates, loads, interrogations, and other DBMS functions operate slowly is vitally important. Such information is best known in advance, so that these operations can be carefully scheduled.

Documentation

Documentation of a database project should not be performed after implementation. If it is, then the application has probably already disintegrated. By the time the documentation is completed users will know what they should and should not have been doing and the realization that the database has failed will already have surfaced.

Since the conceptual specification of the database project is a treaty controlling the behavior of all its users, it must be completed, tested, and debugged before it is put into effect.

The documentation of a database project is in many forms. There are the DBMS reference books, the DBMS and application training guides, internal descriptions, tips and techniques books,

119

traditional application documentation, messages and responses books, and new release information. If all this paper is not planned well in advance and the plan executed with great precision, economy, and order, then a large mess will surely follow. Why not build a database for all these data about the data, and enforce all the rules of database against it as well? Why not implement a metabase?

Training

Training is a process by which knowledge and good practice are transmitted from the teacher to the trainee via some medium. The efficiency of the process is measured by the amount of knowledge and good practice that is exhibited by the trainee.

In general, the lecture approach is both the cheapest and the least efficient. And wouldn't you know, the most effective method--animation--is also the most expensive! A balance can be reached by having the material that changes the most often in lecture form, and the most stable material in animation form.

A real reduction in the cost of animation has come about through the use of Muppets. For example, a Muppet could take a pointer (arrow), bounce along a chain of pointers (CODASYL set) until the right place is found, then take out a set of pliers, pry apart the chain, insert the new link, use the pliers again to close up the chain, take a bow, and then leave. Maybe we could even use Oscar the Grouch as the champion of garbage collection.

The most important part of training is the realization that technicians who train well are rare. That problem can be mitigated somewhat through the use of a training program development, implementation, and maintenance methodology. Further, the methodology must have a way of automatically flagging modules that become out of date. Finally, there must be a method of training trainers to train.

7.7   IMPLEMENTATION PHASE SUMMARY

In ranked order, the most important activities in the implementation phase are logical model validation, data loading and update subsystems, and all the components of system control. Then come hotline, standards, test data, standards, and training. Then, finally, interrogation subsystems. The reason interrogation comes last is because it will only delay the initial operations date of the database project.

7.8 REVIEW QUESTIONS

1. The implementation phase of the database project consists of activities in all four components of database. Briefly list and describe the activities within each component.

2. Define and compare static data model choices to dynamic data model choices.

3. When implementing a database project, what are the major efficiency considerations?

4. What is meant by integrity and a lack of integrity in a database?

5. Why is it essential to analyze thoroughly the storage structure of a DBMS?

6. What is an access strategy? Who is it more important to satisfy, the user or the data processing staff? Why?

7. When is the analysis of the data complete?

8. What are the most important aspects of maintaining the database?

9. Compare the procedures for backup with the procedures for recovery.

10. What major considerations are in order before a reorganization of the database occurs?

11. Describe multiple database processing.

12. Why are security and privacy likely to be more critical for database applications than for other systems?

13. What are the duties of a hotline group, and how would they compare to those of a systems software hotline group?

Implementation Phase

14. What is test data used for?

15. Why is documentation needed? What type is needed for the successful completion of the database project?

8 Production and Administration Phase

Production and administration of the database project comprise activities in four major categories: initial database operations, interrogation development, database application maintenance, and the metabase.

8.1 INITIAL DATABASE OPERATIONS

In the prior phase--implementation--the database subsystems such as update and loading were designed, coded, tested, and debugged, and all the initial data made ready to load. Database operations thus start with the initial database load and then continue with the activation of various update and interrogation subsystems. As the update subsystems come on-line, the system control facilities used to keep the database in optimal condition are also activated. Finally the interrogation subsystems that are part of the initial system are made available to users. Once all these initial systems are in place, the database is operational. Thereafter, the activities center on interrogation development and system design maintenance and evolution.

8.2 INTERROGATION DEVELOPMENT

At this point in the database project, interrogation subsystem development can begin in earnest. Development of database uses should be rather straightforward, because the DBMS utilized for the database definitely makes projects simpler. Removed from the application is a good part of the file definition and interface logic, as well as the file access, blocking, and data translation logic. Remaining are formatting of calculations and output reports. If any significant program logic that was supposed to be removed by the DBMS still remains, then the DBMS is quite deficient.

A significant by-product of the database approach is the lessened dependence on methodologies that analyze, design, and structure the writing of programs.

Development of an interrogation module begins with the development of an output specification. An element analysis of the proposed output leads to an assessment of the amount of processing and the number of transformations required to produce the results. If the report is complex enough, then structured design and programming techniques should be employed. In the event that a natural language is employed, then its language form, liberally interspersed with comment statements, may be sufficient to convey the full meaning of the interrogation.

Certain interrogations are whole subsystems--payroll processing, for example. The process, detailed in the interrogation section of the previous chapter, is complicated enough to benefit from the use of structured techniques.

Once developed, an interrogation should be validated against a test database for two reasons: first, for correct operation; second, for efficient operation. If the interrogation does not operate efficiently, its performance may be improved by changing the way the database is accessed. For example, it may be more efficient to scan a set of records in search of a subset than to use a set of indexes, which when fully resolved point to the same subset of records. Or the converse may be true--or neither may be true.

The performance of an interrogation may also be improved through manipulation of DBMS buffer allocations, of run-unit memory allocations, of DBMS overlay structures, and the like. If the database is not ideally organized, the performance may be improved dramatically through database physical reorganization. For example, if the DBMS's physical record can store an owner and ten related members, but due to significant additions and deletions, five of the related members are stored in different physical records, then the retrieval of an owner and its members might take six to eight input-output (I/O) operations. After physical reorganization the retrieval might take one or two I/Os. That is a three- to eight-fold improvement.

Finally, a small change in the database design might produce dramatic performance improvements. For example, in Figure 2.3, if there were a report that listed all the CONTRACTS for a particular SALESPERSON, CUSTOMER, and REGION, there would be two very different ways to formulate the interrogation. The two ways are illustrated in Figures 8.1 and 8.2 and are coded in a BASIC-like language.

```
   5  FIND REGION EQ "EAST," ON ERROR GOTO 9000
  10  GET SALESPERSON, ON ERROR GOTO 9010
  15  IF SALESPERSON NE "JONES" GOTO 10
  20  GET CUSTOMER, ON ERROR GOTO 9020
  25  IF CUSTOMER NE "AJAX TRACTOR" GOTO 20
  30  GET CONTRACT, ON ERROR GOTO 9030
  35  PRINT CONTRACT-ID, CONTRACT-NAME, TOTAL-ORDER-COST
  40  GET CONTRACT, AT END GOTO 9040
  45  GOTO 35
9000  PRINT "NO REGION FOUND," GOTO 9100
9010  PRINT "NO SALESPERSON FOUND," GOTO 9100
9020  PRINT "NO CUSTOMER FOUND," GOTO 9100
9030  PRINT "NO CONTRACT FOUND," GOTO 9100
9040  PRINT "END OF CONTRACTS"
9100  END
```

Figure 8.1   Record-Processing-Intensive Interrogation

In Figure 8.1, the processing alternative parses the full set of records regardless of whether or not the selected record satisfies the search. If there are 100 salespersons per region and 100 customers per salesperson and 50 contracts per salesperson, it is probable that the interrogation will take--on the average--150 record accesses to produce the report. This alternative is record processing intensive.

The second alternative, coded in Figure 8.2, is to some extent the inverse of the first. It utilizes indexes to locate a set of records that satisfy the requirements. This alternative then is index processing-intensive.

These two alternatives could take different amounts of time, either of which might be acceptable, or both of which might be unacceptable. The first could be unacceptable because it requires that 150 records be accessed to produce the report. The second alternative could be unacceptable for analogous reasons. The index processor might build, normalize, and then resolve lists. While the REGION, SALESPERSON, and CUSTOMER selections each only produce a list of one cell, the REGION would normalize down to the CUSTOMER level, producing a list of 10,000 (1 x 100 x 100) cells. The SALESMAN would normalize down to a 100-cell list. These two lists would have to be ANDed together, which might take considerable CPU time.

```
  5  LOCATE CONTRACT WHERE REGION EQ "EAST" AND
         SALESPERSON EQ "JONES" AND
         CUSTOMER EQ "AJAX TRACTOR,"ON ERROR GOTO 9010
 10  GET CONTRACT, AT END GOTO 9020
 20  PRINT CONTRACT-ID, CONTRACT-NAME, TOTAL-ORDER-COST
 30  GOTO 10
9010  PRINT "NO CONTRACT RECORD FOUND," GOTO 9100
9020  PRINT "END OF CONTRACTS"
9100  END
```

Figure 8.2   List-Processing-Intensive Interrogation

Assuming that both alternatives are unacceptable, the following slight modification of the database should bring about dramatic improvements. Add to the CONTRACT record type the element REGION-SALESPERSON-CUSTOMER, which would contain, for example, the value <EAST JONES AJAX TRACTOR>. Once included in the database, the alternative in Figure 8.2 is modified to that shown in Figure 8.3.

This alternative permits direct access of the correct set of CONTRACTS. Query throughput is dramatically improved. But since nothing is free, the costs are these: .im chaptitl/txt,t0803

- o   An extra element has been added, which requires definition of all appropriate semantics.

- o   The database is no longer completely "natural," since it has become somewhat oriented toward a particular report.

- o   Extra update operations are required to keep the extra element current.

These costs have to be balanced against the benefits obtained from interrogation improvements.

```
   5  LOCATE CONTRACT WHERE REGION-SALESPERSON-CUSTOMER
         EQ "EAST JONES AJAX TRACTOR,"ON ERROR GOTO 9020
  10  GET CONTRACT, AT END GOTO 9020
  30  GOTO 10
9010  PRINT "NO CONTRACT FOUND,"GOTO 9100
9020  PRINT "END OF CONTRACTS"
9100  END
```

Figure 8.3   Modified List-Processing Interrogation

The selection of the right language for an interrogation must be balanced against the performance achieved. If the performance is not acceptable, then another language may have to be used--one that provides greater flexibility in choosing record processing or index processing. Finally, slight changes in the database might be required to achieve acceptable performance.

8.3   DATABASE APPLICATION CHANGE

In general, there are three areas in the database application that can change. These changes relate to the interrogation module, the database application itself, and the database project supports.

Interrogation Changes

Interrogation changes are going to be with us forever. That, of course, is exactly why interrogation should never be on the critical path of a database project.

In the database approach, the promise is that interrogation, and, in turn, changes to interrogations, are easier. Changes are easier because each application no longer includes file definition and interface logic, or file access, blocking, and data translation logic.

In many update and report programs, the number of lines of code that these types of logic require is quite significant--

127

sometimes up to 60%. At a cost of $50.00 per line, a traditional 1000 line program might cost $20,000 rather than $50,000.

Database Application Changes

Changes to the logical database include the addition of new elements, the deletion of elements no longer a viable part of an object's policy, the addition or deletion of relationships, and the like. The effects of these changes depend mainly on whether the DBMS is static or dynamic. If it is static, a design change can cause significant database down time until the change is made. When this rebuilding is required, provisions are usually made to make changes in batch or even to build parallel versions that operate in tandem until the change is completed.

Changes in the physical database are usually undertaken to change the processing efficiency of a certain implementation orientation. Indexes are added or deleted, relationships are made more direct or more indirect, and so on. Since these changes also often require database reloads, the logical and physical database changes are often "batched" together to be accomplished on a specific quarterly or semiannual schedule.

System control changes usually cannot wait. If a design flaw in the integrity of the audit trail is discovered, the database is usually shut down immediately and it does not come back on line until the flaw is fixed.

Support Changes

Support changes affect the manner in which the database environment operates. For example, there might be new or modified training courses, changed documentation standards, new hotline procedures, or more valid and easier-to-use test data.

Database Application Change Summary

The main problem with traditional systems is change. It is estimated that 60 percent of data processing budgets are expended on change. Since less than half of this problem is accounted for by either design changes or DBMS bugs, the majority must be spent to maintain reports. If the database project is defined so as to exclude significant interrogation, and if interrogation can be farmed out to the users who have access to flexible, easy-to-use, easy-to-change languages, then the whole problem of maintenance greatly diminishes.

Interrogation Development

The second type of change relates to DBMS bugs that are handled by the DBMS specialist. If a bug cannot easily be fixed, then an application change may be required to effect a work-around. The third change type relates to design changes. These stem from two sources. The first relates to an improper approach to system design, the second to really legitimate problems. The techniques described in Chapter 6 offer to solve the first type.

The second type of changes, the really legitimate ones, are actually signs of evolution in our understanding of the business. When the application first becomes operational there are only a few change requests, because users are learning the system's capabilities. But as time passes and system usage increases, there are likely to be a significant number of change requests. Once the first round of these changes has been implemented, the next rounds contain fewer requests.

Design changes sometimes affect a large number of data update and reporting programs. Also, some changes require the loaded database to be unloaded and then reloaded. Once the database application is operational, these two change effects (reprogramming and reloading) can be both expensive and time-consuming. It is desirable, therefore, to restrict design changes of an operational database system to changes that are critical or very important.

Database prototyping can be employed to significantly reduce the number of design changes that normally arise shortly after the database system becomes operational. The reduction is accomplished by identifying and resolving the design changes during the conceptual specification phase. During this phase, design changes are quick and easy to incorporate simply because no programs have been written and no data have been collected or loaded. These two activities--programming and data loading--are very time-consuming and expensive, and are the most significant factors to be considered in computing the estimated cost of a database design change.

The process of prototyping is simple. An initial database design is generated and loaded with test data. It is then demonstrated to critical users. As design inaccuracies surface, they are corrected, and a new design is created. The new design is tested; and if any changes are needed they can be made quickly. This process of iterative design is continued until all but the most subtle changes are accomplished. In this way, few, if any, changes to the database are necessary during the initial operations period.

129

As the technique of prototyping improves and becomes more acceptable, the initially implemented database design will more accurately reflect the real environment, which in turn will greatly lessen the number of system design changes.

8.4 THE METABASE

A database project is implemented to automate the storage, update, and reporting of data about a particular corporate function. The database's data, then, are the mechanisms management uses to account for and control this function. Examples of these systems would be personnel management, accounting and finance, and long-range planning. No self-respecting business would exist without these systems that deal with basic functions. Certainly one of business's basic functions is data processing, but seldom are there automated systems to support the basic functions of data processing. A system is needed to store, update, and report on the data that enables management to account for, control, manage, and effectively plan for this critical area of a business's operations. No self-respecting business should exist without such a system--and the metabase system is that system. It is made possible by the database approach, and the best tool for its implementation is the DBMS.

While the metabase system is important for standard data processing systems, it is absolutely critical for database systems. Typically, a database application's documentation exists in at least a dozen large binders, and that does not include the DBMS-related documents or the actual program designs or listings. It is clearly impossible to manage this monumental amount of paper effectively in any unautomated way.

The metabase system must store, update, maintain, report, protect, and preserve all these data in the most accessible form. This is best done with a DBMS. Most DBMS vendors have recognized this fact and have implemented their metabases, also called data dictionaries, using their own DBMS as the main source of power. Typically, vendor-provided metabase packages address only the data processing portion of the metabase requirements, so they must be greatly expanded to include all the artifacts of the database project.

Designs do exist for metadata databases, and there have been some very successful implementations when the following considerations have been kept in mind:

o Canned data dictionary packages or DBMS-based systems must be capable of expanding in terms of data and reports to suit the peculiar needs of the organization.

o Successful metadata database projects require high-level organizational attention, input, review, and guidance--roughly analogous to the effort expended on other critical data processing systems.

o The best results are achieved when the metadata database has been integrated into the work process that designs, implements, maintains, and operates automated systems.

8.5 PRODUCTION AND ADMINISTRATION SUMMARY

While the database approach has not totally alleviated the problems of application maintenance, it has made much of the maintenance easier. It is easier because DBMS eliminates a significant portion of each program. The interrogation languages themselves enhance both development and changes, due to their self-evident form. Finally, the DBMS permits single changes to be made in the affected area without having to change unaffected programs.

The most helpful complement to a database is the metabase. Its development permits data administration to become a reality. Until the metabase is developed, there is nothing that can report on the purpose, intent, cost, and use of automated data. And until that is done, data processing is likely to be viewed as merely a rabid consumer of precious resources that has to be controlled, rather than as a facilitator of enhanced planning and management.

8.6 REVIEW QUESTIONS

1. List the three major components of the maintenance and administration of a database project.

Production and Administration Phase

2. It was stated in the first chapter that the database approach must not be used for process-oriented systems. That statement is generally correct, but give an example of a process that might benefit from database technology.

3. Describe each of the three most common types of application maintenance.

4. Why should not interrogation be on the critical path of a database?

5. Give some examples of database application changes.

6. Explain why the other name for a data dictionary is more appropriate.

7. What must be kept in mind when implementing a metadata database?

8. Within traditional data processing environments, what is the average percentage of the entire data processing budget that is spent on maintenance? Why is this the case?

9. How does database affect maintenance cost estimates?

10. Why is it more important to fix system control problems than interrogation problems?

9 The DBMS Viewpoint

9.1 THE DBMS DICHOTOMY

Chapter 2 presented the technological basis for the database approach, which is almost always implemented in computer software as the database management system (DBMS). This chapter presents DBMSs from the viewpoint of the features that "should" typically be present to support a comprehensive and sophisticated environment.

Users often think that most DBMSs are similar. In fact, they are not. There are very significant differences, and the most important difference is the method by which a DBMS relates records of the same type and records of different types. The static relationship DBMSs relate records by DBMS-generated pointers; the dynamic DBMSs relate records by user-supplied data values that occur in common in the related records.

In general, a static DBMS is one designed to optimize the capture of large volumes of transactions in standard formats and to update a database with these transactions in the most efficient manner.

A static database is one that contains a set of very organized record types, usually with embedded relationship pointers that relate record occurrences. These pointers are present so that production reports and updates--that is, those types of activities which seldom change--can execute efficiently. Once the static database is created, changes to the inter-record relationships normally require a complete database reload.

The DBMS Viewpoint

In contrast, a dynamic DBMS is one that is designed to optimize the processing of unstructured (ad hoc) queries and updates that may involve many selection conditions, DBMS-supported sorting, or the production of sophisticated reports.

The dynamic database is not prestructured into either a network or hierarchy through the use of embedded pointers, as is the static database. Rather, dynamic DBMS interrecord relationships are based solely on common data values that exist in the related records. The users stipulate these relationships, and the dynamic DBMS finds the records that meet the conditions imposed by these stipulated relationships.

In a dynamic database, usually at least 20 percent of the elements are indexed in order to speed the search for records. Because of this heavy use of indexing, the time needed to update is considerable, as all the affected indexes also have to be updated.

The predominant use of a dynamic database is query, with single record type updating, while the predominant use of a static database is production reporting, with complex multiple record type updating.

Clearly, the interrecord relationship is the critical difference between static and dynamic DBMSs. Figure 9.1 contrasts the characteristics of this important difference.

DBMS TYPE (Interrecord relationships)	
STATIC	DYNAMIC
Defined through DDL	Optionally Defined
Created through DBMS	Created through User Defined Field Values
Bound at Load/Update	Bound at Retrieval
Changed through Delete and Re-Add	Changed through Field Update

Figure 9.1   Interrecord Relationships:
Static and Dynamic DBMS Comparison

This chapter presents the (by now) famous four components of database as viewed through the DBMS's colored glass. The appendix contains examples of various DBMSs that are representative of static and dynamic data models.

9.2 THE LOGICAL DATABASE

The DBMS's logical database is a semantic expression of the data elements, records, and relationships. This semantic expression is known as the database's schema. Whether the DBMS is static or dynamic, the definition process itself and the specification of the records and the data elements is the same.

The logical database definition statements are communicated to the DBMS via a data definition language (DDL). It contains all the statements necessary to communicate the complete semantics of the database. The data definition language has traditionally been syntactically oriented. There is no reason however, why it could not be represented through interactive screen displays that accomplish the desired end result. Included in any DDL should be at least the following:

o Schema specification

o Domains

o Record specification

o Data Element specification

o Relationship specifications

o Index specifications

o Subschema specifications

Schema Specification

The schema specification statement states the name of the database.

Domains

A domain contains the specification of the type and value characteristics for a particular data element that might be used in different places throughout the database. For example, sex would have the domain of male and female; and salary would have the domain 3,000 to 60,000.

The types of data that should be included in domains are fixed- and variable-length character strings, single- and multiple-dimension arrays, fixed- and floating-point numbers, integers, and special data types such as date and time.

Finally, each domain should be able to specify a series of statements that govern the values that are allowed in the element. Included should be:

o   Valid value ranges

o   Specific valid values

o   Invalid value ranges

o   Specific invalid values

o   Numbers of occurrences

o   Duplicates allowed or disallowed

o   Default values

o   Conversion rules

o   Null

Record Specifications

A record type, in the context of a DBMS, is a collection of defined data elements. A DBMS allows record occurrences, represented by the record type, to be inserted, deleted, and sorted, and to be related to record instances of the same and different types.

From the DBMS view, the record occurrence is purely technical. Thus, if the record is to be a statement of management policy, all that work has to be done well in advance of the DBMS's deployment.

The record clause part of the record's definition should contain the name of the record and any collection of computable rules that govern the acceptance or rejection of the data record as a whole. For example, record insertion might be denied if all the elements are not valued or if HIRE-DATE is less than the BIRTH-DATE or greater than the DEATH-DATE.

An example of the record type SALESPERSON is depicted in Figure 9.2. In the instance of a record type definition, the record name is EMPLOYEE; and on the DML verb STORE, the procedure STORE-REC-PROC is invoked to process the record before its actual inclusion in the database. The DBMS will not allow duplicates for this record type in the database. The DBMS is instructed by the DDL to build indexes for SSN, JOB-TITLE, and REGION. Finally, the data elements in the record type include SSN, EMPLOYEE-NAME, etc.

The Logical Database

The actual data that is represented by a record type's definition is called a record instance. A record instance for the record type defined in Figure 9.2 might be:

249245300|John Monahan|Manager|North East|....

In this example, the "|" symbol is employed to illustrate field value separation.

Data Element Specifications

Included with each record specification should be a set of data element clauses. Each data element clause should be able to incorporate by reference the specifications contained in a domain specification, and be able to change or augment them. Generally, the five types of data elements are: single valued, multiple valued, multiple dimension, group, and repeating group.

```
RECORD IS SALESPERSON;
ON STORE, CALL STORE-REC-PROC;
INDEXES ARE SSN, JOB-TITLE, REGION;
DUPLICATES NOT ALLOWED;
FIELD IS SSN; TYPE IS...;...
FIELD IS EMPLOYEE-NAME; TYPE IS...;...
FIELD IS JOB-TITLE; TYPE IS...;...
FIELD IS REGION; TYPE IS...;...
             .
             .
             .
RECORD IS....
```

Figure 9.2 Salesperson Record Type Definition

Because the data element specification is now within the context of a record, condition clauses included in the data element specification should be able to include other elements in the record's definition.

The definition construct of an element is called an element type. Figure 9.3 contains an example of the DDL for the data element JOB-TITLE. A valid element occurrence of the JOB-TITLE type would be SENIOR. In this element, across all record instances in which this element occurs, duplicate values are allowed, and an invalid occurrence would be JUNIOR, or "blank."

Most data elements are single valued. In the case of a product database, the element PRODUCT-NAME would only have one value. Some other element types are multiple valued with only one dimension, as in SALES-BY-MONTH, which would have 12 values for each product record. Still others have multiple dimensions, as in SALES-BY-MONTH-BY-YEAR, which might be 120 values, that is, 12 per year for 10 years for each product record.

Some records allow the definition of groups. A group has a name, and then a set of individually defined elements, which may act as a redefinition. For example, FULL-NAME might be redefined into FIRST-NAME, MI, and LAST-NAME. Finally, the record may allow the group to contain multiple occurrences (repeating group). For example, there might be a discount struc-ture for product sales. For each DISCOUNT, there might be a QUANTITY-MINIMUM element, a QUANTITY-MAXIMUM element, and a PRICE element. In some DBMSs, a repeating group is additionally allowed to contain multi-valued items and other repeating groups.

FIELD IS JOB-TITLE; TYPE IS CHAR; LENGTH IS 10;
NULL IS NOT ALLOWED; DUPLICATES ARE ALLOWED;
VALID VALUES ARE SENIOR, TRAINEE, MANAGER.

Figure 9.3   Job Title Data Element Definition

When the DBMS allows only single-valued elements in each record, then its record types are simple. When multi-valued elements, groups, and so on, are allowed, the record structure is said to be complex.

Complex Record Types.   Some DBMSs allow record types of such complexity that to distinguish record types from dependent structures within a record type is difficult. For example, SYSTEM 2000's hierarchical data model permits any reasonable number of repeating groups on any level, and up to 32 levels. Is the repeating group a record type in its own right, or is it a dependent segment within a record type? The following guideline should help establish the difference:

> A record type can be stored, retrieved, and deleted on its own, independently from others, while dependent segments need the location and context of others for their own storage, retrieval, and deletion.

A DBMS record type almost always has a defined primary key with all dependent segments defined in subordinate roles, and when the record is deleted (after being selected by means of its primary key), all dependent segments are also deleted. In contrast, a dependent segment does not require a primary key of its own, especially in information-bearing relationships, because the dependent segment is accessed from within the context of a record that has a key. Further, the dependent segment can be deleted without affecting the higher level record type. However, its deletion often affects lower level segments that may be defined in a subordinate relationship to the segment being deleted.

A SYSTEM 2000 implementation of the structure in Figure 2.4 results in two databases, each having one record type. The first record type has six segments, and the second has four. Each has only one record type because a delete operation to remove an instance of the COMPANY also removes all instances of the COMPANY's dependent segments. PRODUCT, PRODUCT SPECIFICATION, PRODUCT PRICE, REGION, and SALESPERSON are also deleted.

An IDMS database implementation of Figure 2.3 can be either as a single database with a set of simple independent record types, or as a single database that contains several complex record types along with several simple record types. The segments that are related hierarchically can be implemented as independent simple record types or as dependent segments with complex record types. The database designer must define formal relationships (sets) to relate independent record types. No formal relationships have to be defined to relate dependent segments. Formally defined relationships (sets) can only be defined between and among record types, not among dependent segments.

The ANSI X3H2's network data language (NDL) data model permits each record type to have simple fields and a multi-dimensional field. The model does not allow for formally defined single value groups such as ADDRESS, which would contain the subordinate fields for STREET, CITY, STATE, and ZIP. Nor does the model allow for repeat value groups such as DEPENDENTS, which would contain multiple occurrences of FIRST-NAME, BIRTH-DATE, and SEX. Finally, the model does not allow nested repeating groups such as a HOBBIES group defined within DEPENDENTS group. The rationale behind this simpler record type structure was that these types of groups cannot be rigorously distinguished in existing ANSI languages such as COBOL or FORTRAN. A beneficial side effect of the simpler record type structure is that the ANSI network record type is similar to the relational database standard that is also under development by X3H2.

In some static DBMSs, record types that have complex subordinate structures can have the segments belonging to the subordinate structures--for example, the DISCOUNT segment, stored noncontiguously from the main part of the PRODUCT record. These noncontiguous segments are connected by DBMS-generated addresses. Consequently, a complex record type, which in turn implies a significant amount of data (maybe 5000 characters), can be stored in a computer-efficient manner.

In dynamic DBMSs, the record occurrence is normally stored in contiguous space. Because of this, and for reasons described in the relationship specification section below, most dynamic DBMS record types are simple. Some, however, are complex, but they typically allow only one level of repeating groups in order to have record occurrences that can be stored in a computer-efficient manner. Dynamic DBMSs thus have either simple records or complex ones with one nested level.

Relationship Specifications

The DBMS should allow for the establishment of named association of two or more record types. It should also allow multiple relationships between one owner and one member type and between multiple member types.

In Figure 9.4, which depicts an ANSI network data model structure, the obvious relationship between REGION and SALESPERSON could be named BELONGS-TO. That is, a salesperson belongs to a particular region. Other relationships might also be SENIOR-SALESPERSON, QUOTA-ACHIEVERS, and the like.

Another type of relationship is called recursive. That is, the owner and the member records are of the same type. For example, one salesperson may be the boss of the others. The relationship BOSS would then have SALESPERSON as both its owner and member record type. One salesperson would be identified as the owner (boss), and the others would be classified as members.

A third type of relationship is the multiple member. That is, two or more record types are members within the same relationship, for example, TERRITORY. It links REGION, SALESPERSON and CUSTOMERS in a single relationship. The region record would be initially retrieved, then the first salesperson, and then the customers assigned the salesperson. When there are no more customers, the next salesperson would be retrieved. When all the salespersons have been exhausted, all the territories in the region will have been traversed. A DDL for this multiple member relation is contained in Figure 9.5.

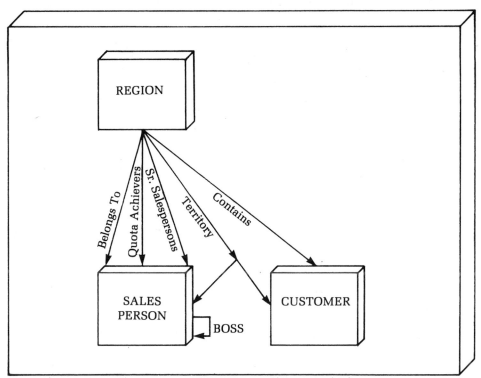

Figure 9.4   ANSI Network Data Model

An instance of the TERRITORY relationship (see Figure 9.4) is an instance of the mechanism that relates a specific REGION occurrence to specific occurrences of SALESPERSON and CUSTOMER. Note that the instance of a relationship is not a set of record instances from the record types that participate in the relationship, even though such a set of record types is normally the visual mechanism for viewing a relationship instance. Rather, the relationship instance is the set of pointers that bind the record instances together in the relationship.

These and other relationship types are almost the exclusive domain of the ANSI network data model. The hierarchical data model can have only one relationship between record types. Further, it is the responsibility of the user to know of and enforce owner-member integrity constraints. The dynamic data models also do not have explicit relationships, but at least relationships among record types are determinable on the basis of commonly shared element values.

Static and Dynamic Relationship Differences. There are two methods by which a DBMS "knows" of a relationship: static and dynamic. The static relationship, created by the DBMS, is usually represented by a relative record address. This address, that points "to" a particular record, is most often stored in the "from" record. A dynamic relationship, created by the user, is usually a duplicated data value stored in the records that participate in the relationship.

```
RELATIONSHIP IS TERRITORY
    OWNER IS REGION:
        ORDER IS SALESPERSON, CUSTOMER;
    MEMBER IS SALESPERSON:
        DUPLICATES PROHIBITED;
        KEY IS SALESPERSON-ID;
        CONNECTION RULES ARE
            ASSIGN-DATE GE EMP-HIRE-DATE,
            ASSIGN-DATE LE EMP-TERM-DATE;
    MEMBER IS CUSTOMER;
        DUPLICATES PROHIBITED;
        KEY IS CUSTOMER-ID.
```

Figure 9.5 Static DDL for Territory Relationship

It is important to understand that the relationship that binds records together may or may not also reflect their physical order. For example, if employee records are physically stored in the database in the order of their birth, then a sequential access of the database will also represent a chronological access. However, if employees are stored in a physical sequence that is EMPLOYEE-ID order, as illustrated in Figure 9.6, then it is very unlikely that a sequential access will produce records in FULL-NAME alphabetical order. To accomplish the alphabetical order report, either the records must be removed and sorted or there must be a separately maintained association among the records that is utilized for record access.

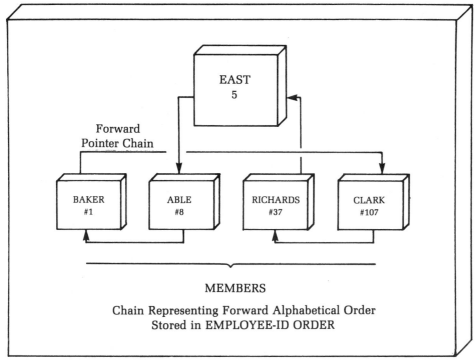

Figure 9.6 Physical Form of a Relationship

This alphabetical association can be represented as relative record address pointers that are stored in the records. The association is easiest to create when the DBMS initially stores the records. Upon storage, the record's address and the alphabetical value of FULL-NAME on which the sort is to be based is stored by the DBMS in a temporary work file. At the end of the load, the temporary work file is sorted by the DBMS by the FULL-NAME alphabetical key order. The records can then be accessed by the DBMS in alphabetical order via the sorted set of record addresses. The pointer space within the record that is used for chaining to the "next" record is filled with the address of the "next" record and then the record is written back to the database. This DBMS process of record access and "next" record address storage is continued until the DBMS accesses and stores the alphabetical sequence of pointers in all the records. The final record, depending on the DBMS, usually contains a special flag to indicate "end-of-chain," or points back to the owner.

After initial loading, the order can be maintained by first storing the new record, then accessing the existing records in alphabetical chain order until the record is found that represents the immediately preceeding alphabetical record. Next, the address of the newly stored record is used to replace the address of the existing "next" pointer in the alphabetically preceeding record. Finally, the "old" next pointer is stored in the new record.

Traditionally, these pointers are stored in the records. However, they might be stored in structures separated from the records, commonly called pointer arrays. Regardless of how these pointers are stored, relationships represent mechanisms of associations among record occurrences that may have little or nothing to do with the actual location of stored records. This would certainly be true if the "pointers" that point from one record to another in the relationship chain were primary-key values such as EMPLOYEE-ID. If all the EMPLOYEE-IDs were stored in an array, having been first sorted by the alphabetical key, then when an EMPLOYEE-ID was accessed, it would be used to locate and access the record.

The value of having data values instead of record addresses as relationship mechanisms is that database records can be relocated without having to modify these relationship pointer addresses. On the negative side, since the data value does not point directly to the location of the record, an extra database access is needed to determine the record's location and then retrieve it.

That the mechanism of relationship is a data value doesn't automatically mean that the relationship is dynamic. In the case described above, the relationship is clearly static, for two reasons. First, the EMPLOYEE-ID value is intended solely to represent the alphabetical association of one record to the next. Second, when a record is removed, the alphabetical association among the records is "broken." It is "broken" when a record is removed because the removed record's prior alphabetically related record, which contains the primary key of the removed record as its next pointer, now points to nothing, and the record after the one removed, which contains the primary key of the removed record as its prior pointer, also points to nothing. In short, because of the deleted record, an alphabetical scan is not possible. Thus, the relationship is "broken." Additionally, when a new record is added, the dynamic DBMS has no mechanism to add the record's EMPLOYEE-ID to the alphabetically sorted list of record keys.

If the DBMS possesses the mechanisms to add, delete, and repair relationship links (whether pointer or data value) then the DBMS is certainly static. Without these mechanisms the DBMS is dynamic and must possess linguistic facilities to discover which records participated in the relationship.

Static Relationships. Static DBMS relationships are fast to traverse, but slow to change. There are three types of changes: add, delete, and modify. To add a relationship reference to a record such that the record now participates in a relationship, the user must employ data manipulation language (DML) verbs to locate the proper position within the relationship chain, and then issue the DML verb that causes the relationship references in the surrounding records to be modified to reflect the addition of the record's relationship reference. The relationship deletion operation is the inverse of the add operation. The modify operation is the combination of the delete operation and then the add operation.

Because it is simpler to conceptualize a chain of records linked along a relationship (see Figure 9.7) than a set of relationships linked along a set of stored records (see Figure 9.6), and to use expressions like insert, delete, or modify a record into a relationship instead of using expressions like insert, delete, or modify a relationship pointer into a set of records, the remainder of this book describes relationship operations in terms of record operations.

As a brief review, as illustrated in Figures 9.6 and 9.7, the collection of static relationships that bind records is often called a chain. The head of the chain--that is, the start of the linked relationship--is known as the owner. In the owner record there is a pointer that allows the DBMS to find the first member. In the first member there is a pointer that refers to the next member, and so forth. In the last member, there is normally a pointer that refers back to the owner. In this case, the chain forms a ring. Some relationships also have prior and owner pointers.

The DBMS Viewpoint

The DBMS's relationship specification clauses should be able to have clauses to state whether new records are stored automatically at the front of the chain, at the end of the chain, or in sorted order. When the DBMS automatically sorts the relationships that represent the records, the DDL sort clause should contain one or more elements to serve as sort keys. The sort clauses should clearly state how duplicate values for the combined sort keys are handled, that is, whether they are stored at the head or tail of the chain, or rejected altogether.

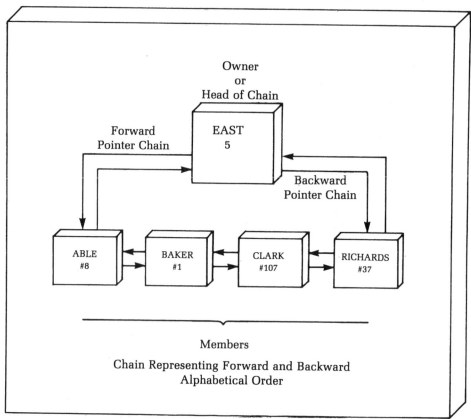

Figure 9.7 Logical Form of a Relationship

A most important static relationship clause pertains to record insertion and retention in both the database and the relationship. Clauses should allow the record to be automatically stored in the database, to be put off into a temporary location for later connection into the relationship, or to be deleted from the relationship but not from the database.

146

The Logical Database

For example, in Figure 2.3, ORDERS and CONTRACTS are bound together through the relationship of contracts containing orders. It would certainly be illogical to be able to DELETE a CONTRACT and leave the ORDER record types in the database. The DBMS should either prevent the deletion of CONTRACT record through the use of a retention clause or automatically delete the ORDER records when the CONTRACT record is deleted. Of course, if the ORDER record is deleted, then the ORDER-ITEM records should also be automatically deleted. In the hierarchical data model the deletion of an owner record type automatically deletes its members. In the dynamic data models, member records remain in the database since the owner does not know of the member's existence.

Static DBMSs have this large collection of record relationship and integrity clauses; thus, they cause the data to be highly organized. All the records are stored in a very specific order and can be retrieved only in that order. If there is to be any other order, the records must first be removed, placed in an external file, and sorted.

For the application whose processing logic is the same as the organization of the database, the application is very efficient. For the application whose processing logic is inverse to the database design, either the application cannot be carried out, or it can be done only very slowly, or it will require complete database reorganization and reloading before it is efficient--for that new set of reports. And when another new set of reports comes along the process just described begins again.

Dynamic Relationships. Some DBMSs can determine that relationships exist among records of the same or different types dynamically. These records are related through common element values. The owner-member relationship is accomplished by having an element value, which occurs in only one owner-type record, occur in multiple member records. In Figure 2.5, for example, if the REGION-NUMBER value is repeated in each of the SALESPERSON's records, when a request is initiated to locate all owners and members with a particular REGION-NUMBER value, the region and the salespersons are selected. Since in a dynamic relationship there is no predetermined order to the records, nor do any records belong to a relationship in a way that is "known" to either the "owner" or to a prior member, then every natural language or host language interrogation has an equal basis for efficiency.

147

The DBMS Viewpoint

If there is a requirement for an alphabetically sorted list of records, then the requestor activates a SORT verb that extracts the record key and the value upon which the sort is to be performed, sorts the record keys into the order of the extracted values, and then proceeds to retrieve the records by the sorted key.

Most dynamic DBMSs do not allow for the formal expression of relationships through DDL. Rather, the burden of knowing about the relationships and the burden of knowing how to express a relationship between record types is left to the query language user.

A dynamic DBMS might allow the expression of the relationships and the record presentation sort orders that are to govern specific interrogations from within the context of a subschema. Two examples are contained in Figure 9.8.

The actual order of the records in the database is not known, and for a dynamic DBMS this order is irrelevant, since the dynamic DBMS can cause these records to be presented in any order that can be determined on the basis of some element value--SALESPERSON-ID, CUSTOMER-ID, SALESPERSON-HIRE-DATE, and CUSTOMER-TOTAL-PURCHASES.

It needs to be pointed out that the relationships as well as the sort order contained in Figure 9.8 were specified in the subschema. Thus, the subschema specified relationships have an effect on the program that utilizes them for record selection and presentation, not on the DBMS which "controls" record storage in the database. The effect is that there is less user programming required, since the DBMS takes charge of and accomplishes these programming requests.

The fact that these two facilities--relationships and order--are specified in the subschema merely serves to save key strokes over their specification within the interrogation languages. These facilities certainly should be able to be specified within an interrogation.

In relational terminology, the subschema is a view. In some dynamic DBMS's, the subschema/view is specified through a formal DDL process much the same as in a static DBMS. In some other dynamic DBMS's, the subschema/view is defined at the time of interrogation, and is often able to be stored and reused during that query session. Some relational DBMSs allow record selection and sorting logic to be defined as part of the view. These stored views can then be invoked--one after another--to iteratively subset the database data until the desired result is achieved.

148

Index Specifications

DBMSs should have no practical limit on the number of indexes allowed in each record type. It should be possible to declare that at least one of these indexes requires unique values for elements to serve as unique record identifiers, such as SALESPERSON-ID. Other elements should also be indexable to provide access to collections of records on the basis of a common element value. For example, DEGREE EQ "MA" or SALARY GT "40000".

In a dynamic DBMS, indexes are often the mechanism to relate record occurrences of different types, at query time, on the basis of common element values, just as if they had been joined by an embedded owner-member pointer as in a static database.

```
RELATIONSHIP IS TERRITORY
    OWNER IS REGION:
        ORDER IS SALESPERSON, CUSTOMER;
    MEMBER IS SALESPERSON:
        CONNECTION IS REGION-NUMBER =
            SALESPERSON-REGION-NUMBER
        KEY IS SALESPERSON-ID;
    MEMBER IS CUSTOMER:
        CONNECTION IS SALESPERSON-ID =
            CUSTOMER-SALESPERSON-ID;
        KEY IS CUSTOMER-ID.


RELATIONSHIP IS TERRITORY-CUSTOMER-VALUE
    OWNER IS REGION:
        ORDER IS SALESPERSON, CUSTOMER;
    MEMBER IS SALESPERSON:
        CONNECTION IS REGION-NUMBER =
            SALESPERSON-REGION-NUMBER;
        KEY IS SALESPERSON-HIRE-DATE;
    MEMBER IS CUSTOMER:
        CONNECTION IS SALESPERSON-ID =
            CUSTOMER-SALESPERSON-ID;
        KEY IS CUSTOMER-TOTAL-PURCHASES.
```

Figure 9.8 Dynamic DDL for Territory Relationships

The DBMS Viewpoint

Subschema Specifications

A DBMS should have a subschema facility that enables the DBA to define a user-database interface. The subschema is most often a portion of a schema that includes some record types, some element types, and certain relationships that are relevant to a specific user. The subschema should contain two kinds of user-language specifications: independent and dependent.

Independent Specifications. The independent specifications should include the subschema name, an enumeration of the record names from the schema that belong in the subschema, and an enumeration of the elements from the schema to be used within the subschema records.

Dependent Specifications. The dependent specifications relate directly to the interrogation language. The areas of dependency relate data types, conversion rules, names, natural languages, and relationships.

Data Types. Each language may support data types different from those supported by the DBMS. Rules must be created to allow for the proper translation of the database data types to the language data type. For example, data might be stored in the database in packed decimal format to save space, but FORTRAN can understand only integer and floating point. Thus, the DBMS would have to convert the data from packed decimal to integer or floating point.

Conversion Rules. A database might be able to store double precision floating-point numbers or numbers in scientific notation. For COBOL, the numbers may have to be converted to allow for their use. While the rules for conversion are certainly not within the province of the subschema, statements about the precision of the conversion need to be made.

Names. Each language requires different conventions for names. For example, if COBOL were the language, and if the schema names were multiple words without hyphens, then COBOL would not understand them. On the other hand, if FORTRAN were the language, and the names had hyphens, FORTRAN would interpret the hyphens as minus signs. The rules for natural language names vary from no blanks allowed in names to blanks allowed, to hyphens interpreted as minuses, and so on. The sub-

150

schema should have a well-defined set of alias clauses to over-come these anomalies.

Natural Languages.   Natural languages may also allow the subschema to define default formats for titles, spacing, edit masks, default values for blanks, null values, and so on.

Relationships.   The subschema should be able to specify certain global relationship processing rules for both static and dynamic relationship DBMSs. For static databases that contain multiple relationships between an owner and a member, there should be a statement that names the relationship that is fol-lowed when the language executes a GET MEMBER command.

For dynamic databases, natural language users might appre-ciate their options being limited, while others might require that all options of relationship selection be available.

Logical Database Summary

The logical database for the DBMS is the codification of several distinct types of statements, including record types, element types, and in the case of a static DBMS, relationships. Taken together, the collection of statements is called a schema. A final step in creating the logical database is defining the sub-schemata, which are the interfaces between application programs (HLI or NL) and the DBMS.

Creating the data definition language for a database is like creating source statements for a computer program. If significant analysis and design are conducted prior to programming, the resultant program is likely to be of high quality. In the same way, the database's quality will be directly proportional to the analysis and design effort that precedes schema coding.

9.3   PHYSICAL DATABASE

The physical database consists of five subparts: storage struc-ture, access strategy, data loading, data update, and database maintenance.

Storage Structure

The DBMS's storage structure is the physical organization of the files that constitute a specific database. It normally consists of four components: dictionary, indexes, relationships, and data.

The DBMS Viewpoint

The dictionary contains the loaded and compiled version of the DDL. Indexes are the method for accessing records. Indexes are usually in a primary (no repeated values) or secondary (repeated values allowed) form. Relationships are the mechanisms for relating records of the same type or different types. Data are the actual data records that are stored in the database.

Static Storage Structures. Most static DBMSs have a storage structure that consists of only a few files: one for the dictionary, and a few at most for any indexes, relationships, and data. The storage structure of the relationships and data are usually tightly interwoven. This is because static DBMSs have relationships as an integral part of the data storage area.

To maximize efficiency, some DBMSs allow the storage of specified record types in the same physical file. This enables, for example, members to be as physically close as possible to their owners.

The actual physical record format typically has the physical record (page) broken into two parts. The first part is for the storage of primary key values and addresses of the start of the record, and the second part is for the storage of the actual records. This allows for the contraction and expansion of records within the page.

Most static DBMSs provide for the inclusion of a free space in the physical record to allow for the inclusion of future records. Once the space is gone, the page usually splits, with half of the records, keys, and a pointer to the extra page staying in the original record, and the remainder of the data and keys going into the new page.

The main benefit to be realized by a highly organized static storage structure is the efficient production of reports. When a report is needed, a single physical disk access is likely to obtain a majority of the records needed for a single logical sequence of owner and members.

Dynamic Storage Structure. The dynamic DBMS's storage structure is designed to give each interrogation an equal chance at efficiency. To achieve this performance neutrally, the dynamic DBMS is likely to have a single file for the dictionary, one or more files for the indexes, and one or more files for each dynamic record type.

Record storage is more often in a primary-key value sequence than in a random order, although the latter access strategy is sometimes used. The physical record normally contains a number of records and again some extra space to allow for individual record expansion.

Storage Structure Summary.   The main difference between the static and dynamic DBMS storage structures is that the static structure is designed to give a tremendous boost in efficiency to a certain kind of report processing. The dynamic structure, on the other hand, is ready for any interrogation that comes along; that is, it has no structural orientation toward any particular type of report. For applications in which no type of report predominates, this neutrality is highly desirable. For the application in which certain report operations are executed often, a storage structure that allows record type organizations that favor these reports is highly desirable.

Access Strategy

The access strategy of a DBMS is the method through which the DBMS accesses data records in the database. As might be expected, the general method by which the static and the dynamic database accomplishes record access is quite different. In some DBMSs, the access strategy can be navigated by user language verbs, for example, GET-MEMBER or GET-OWNER. In other DBMSs, the access strategy is controlled by the DBMS, for example, FIND SALESPERSON WHERE REGION EQ "EAST".

Static Access Strategy.   The access strategy of a static DBMS is normally user-directable. That is, the user, through DML verbs, selects the record types to access, selects the sequence for examining the records, and selects the interrecord relationship the DBMS is to resolve.

The user can direct so much because a great majority of the database processing is through a host language. Initial access is usually through a primary key; then, through a series of GET MEMBER, GET NEXT, and GET OWNER commands, the database is traversed until all the data are accumulated for the report or until all the updates are completed.

A command that is often used is the FIND <record-type> <selection-expression>. It allows for the statement of a complex selection expression, which, after processing, returns a subset of record pointers for processing.

The DBMS specialist must select the access strategy for each database. The selection must then be explained to the database specialist so that judgment can be rendered on the

153

correctness of the access when measured against user interrogation and update requirements.

Using the database structure contained in Figure 2.3, the access strategy might be as follows. All record types are direct access except for ORDER, PRODUCT-SPECIFICATION, PRODUCT-PRICE, and ORDER-ITEM. Direct access means that the record is retrieved directly on the basis of its key. Generally, no records are scanned to find the target record; it is found directly.

The PRODUCT-SPECIFICATION, PRODUCT-PRICE, and ORDER-ITEM records are stored "VIA." The term "VIA" means that the records are stored within the same physical record as their via-record-name or as near that record as is possible. When a record is stored VIA, then the pointer stored within its principal owner that points to the VIA record contains a page address that is very likely the same as the owner's. If a record is VIA to one record, it cannot be VIA to another. That means, for example, that ORDER-ITEM cannot be VIA within the relationship that goes from PRODUCT-PRICE to ORDER-ITEM. The relationship between two or more direct access records means that the owner record contains the address of the member. That address, of course, is a direct address, and most often a page-address value different from the owner page-address.

The hierarchical DBMS access strategies are much more straightforward. In Figure 2.4, the owners and members are already set out. Generally, in a hierarchical DBMS, a specific record can be accessed by a primary key such as CUSTOMER-ID. A selection of records can be found through a secondary key like the STATE location for a CUSTOMER. Beyond this general access strategy similarity, IMS and SYSTEM 2000 differ significantly. These differences are not important enough to explore in this book, however.

Dynamic Access Strategy. In contrast to almost complete user control of database navigation, the dynamic DBMS automatically performs most of the navigation and sorting whenever natural language interrogations are provided to the DBMS by users.

The user constructs a selection clause that often has the following form:

TABULATE   <element-list-1>   SORTED   BY   <element-list-2>
        WHERE <selection clause>.

Physical Database

The <element-list-1> may include data elements from the same record type or from multiple record types. The sort clause (<element-list-2>) may include multiple sort keys, in ascending and descending sequences. And the selection expression may include elements from different record types, with conditions involving Boolean operators, relational operators, ranges, and so on.

Often the multiple record type interrogations are resolved through a series of query-time specified record-type-connection clauses that accomplish relationship traversal.

Some dynamic DBMSs determine the lowest node in the selection network and build a completely normalized record type at that level, with the resultant records passing through the various selection criteria. Finally, a set of records are found that fit the selection criteria. They are in turn examined to see if they contain all the criteria for the sort clauses. If not, additional data elements are collected so that the records can be sorted. Once sorted, report formatting is started.

The subschema is examined for any default report formats that may have been specified. If none were, then the interrogation is responsible for supplying all the necessary information. Finally, with all the bureaucracy accomplished, the report is produced. The steps just described all take place automatically and without user involvement subsequent to the submission of the interrogation.

As might be expected, the amount of DBMS and database specialist involvement in the specification of the dynamic DBMS access strategy is quite small. Generally, the specification is limited to determining whether a record is to be independent or a repeating group within another record. Figure 2.5 illustrates both tactics. The only other activity includes determining which element is the primary key and which are the secondary keys.

Comparing Access Strategies. The main difference between the static and dynamic DBMS access strategies is the extent to which navigation control is available to the user. In the static DBMS environment, most of the structure definition decisions are already made on behalf of the user. The languages therefore only provide commands for the preordained, step-by-step navigation of the database's predefined structure.

For example, in Figure 2.3, if a user wanted to know if any salespersons were born in the same town that manufactures a product that the salesperson sold, then the static DBMS typically would help only by providing the salesperson to product links. The program would first have to retrieve a SALESPERSON and then traverse the structure by passing through the CONTRACT, ORDER, ORDER-ITEM, PRODUCT-SPECIFICATION, and finally to PRODUCT to determine whether the product was manufactured in the same town in which the salesperson was born. If the search is successful, elements from the product and salesperson records can be placed on a list in preparation for the report. Then the next ORDER-ITEM can be checked. When the ORDER-ITEMs are exhausted for an ORDER, the next ORDER is checked. That in turn causes the ORDER-ITEM check to begin again. When the ORDERs are exhausted, the next CONTRACT is retrieved and the ORDER check cycle is begun. When all CONTRACTs are exhausted, the next SALESPERSON is retrieved, and then the CONTRACT check cycle begins again. In an abbreviated and rough pseudo-code, the program might be as shown in Figure 9.9.

```
10   SELECT SALESPERSON, ON ERROR GOTO 100, AT END GOTO 110
20   GET MEMBER CONTRACT, ON ERROR GOTO 100, AT END GOTO 10
30   GET MEMBER ORDER, ON ERROR GOTO 100, AT END GOTO 20
40   GET MEMBER ORDER-ITEM, ON ERROR GOTO 100, AT END GOTO 30
50   GET OWNER PRODUCT-SPECIFICATION, ON ERROR GOTO 100
60   GET OWNER PRODUCT, ON ERROR GOTO 100
70   IF PRODUCT-MFG-CITY EQ SALESPERSON-BIRTH-CITY AND
       PRODUCT-MFG-STATE EQ SALESPERSON-BIRTH-STATE
       THEN PRINT SALESPERSON-NAME, PRODUCT-NAME,
       SALESPERSON BIRTH-CITY, SALESPERSON-BIRTH-STATE
       ELSE GOTO 40
100  PRINT "ERROR"
110  END
```

Figure 9.9   A Static Access Strategy Program

In contrast, in the dynamic access strategy, the expression of relationships that create interrecord structures during the query's execution is the responsibility of the user. Once these relationships are expressed by the user, the DBMS translates the relationship expressions into search strategies to accomplish all the navigation, record selection, and sorting automatically, presenting the user with the results.

Physical Database

For example, in Figure 2.6, the static problem described above might be coded as shown in Figure 9.10.

It is important to note that even though the number of statements is roughly the same, the process and mechanism of search are quite different. In the static example, every record between SALESPERSON and PRODUCT is scanned in search of a match.

In the dynamic example, LIST-1 is derived directly, without retrieving records in PRODUCT-SPECIFICATIONS. LIST-2 and LIST-3 are the result of traditional connections. The match between LIST-1 and LIST-3 immediately produces the set of matches at one time, rather than iteratively as in the static example.

In the dynamic example, the generation of interim work files called lists is unique. Once these files are created, some DBMSs allow them to be used completely outside the environment of the database. The DBMS, in turn, is free to service other requests such as updates.

```
10  CONNECT PRODUCT TO ORDER-ITEM
        VIA PRODUCT-NBR EQ ORDER-ITEM-PRODUCT-NBR
20  FIND MATCH AND KEEP PRODUCT-NAME, ORDER-ID,
        PRODUCT-MFG-CITY, PRODUCT-MFG-STATE IN LIST-1
30  CONNECT SALESPERSON TO CONTRACT
        VIA SALESPERSON-NBR EQ CONTRACT-SALESPERSON-ID
40  FIND MATCH AND KEEP SALESPERSON-NAME, CONTRACT-ID,
        SALESPERSON-BIRTH-CITY, SALESPERSON-BIRTH-STATE
        IN LIST-2
50  CONNECT LIST-2 TO ORDER VIA CONTRACT-ID OF LIST-2
        EQ ORDER-CONTRACT-ID
60  FIND MATCH AND KEEP ORDER-ID, SALESPERSON-NAME,
        SALESPERSON-BIRTH-CITY, SALESPERSON-BIRTH-STATE
        IN LIST-3
70  CONNECT LIST-1 TO LIST-3
        VIA ORDER-ID OF LIST-1 EQ ORDER-ID OF LIST-3 AND
        SALESPERSON-BIRTH-CITY EQ PRODUCT-MFG-CITY AND
        SALESPERSON-BIRTH-STATE EQ PRODUCT-MFG-STATE
80  FIND MATCH AND PRINT SALESPERSON-NAME, PRODUCT-NAME,
        SALESPERSON-BIRTH-CITY, SALESPERSON-BIRTH-STATE
```

Figure 9.10 A Dynamic Access Strategy Program

The DBMS Viewpoint

Data Loading

Data loading is the process of bulk loading data into the database. Most DBMSs have specialized utilities to accomplish this task. Data loading is differentiated from the task of data update mainly because data loading is for large amounts of data, while data update is for ongoing data maintenance.

Static Data Loading. Static DBMSs require that the database be loaded according to the dictates of the structure. That is, the owner is loaded first, then its members, then their members. All the other owners to which a member is to be connected are then loaded. An already connected member is then accessed and connected into relationships with its other owners. An alternative loading strategy would be to load all the owners, then load a member and connect it to all its owners.

The process of loading a complicated static network database is complex. Its complexity is directly related to the number of relationships. Once loaded, however, the static database is ready for its high-velocity reporting and updating. That's when the complexity and effort required for loading pays off.

The loading sequence for the record types contained in Figure 2.3, in conjunction with the defined access strategy, would be as follows. This example assumes that records from all types are available and have been properly loaded onto files that are accessible to the data loading program, and that all records are automatically inserted into their proper relationships when sufficient information is available. The record-loading sequence for one natural hierarchy is COMPANY, PRODUCT, PRODUCT-SPECIFICATION, PRODUCT PRICE. The record-loading sequence for the other natural hierarchy is REGION, SALESPERSON, CUSTOMER, CONTRACT, ORDER, and ORDER ITEM.

So far, the loading has been hierarchical. To create the network connections, say for CONTRACT and SALESPERSON, there must be a way to determine which salesperson is to be connected to which contract. If the SALESPERSON-ID is also present in the CONTRACT record, then the specific salesperson is identified and retrieved. Upon retrieval, the relationship instance that binds a SALESPERSON instance and CONTRACT instances together is also made available for parsing. Assuming that the contract is to be stored either as the NEXT, FIRST, or LAST instance within the set, this same process is performed to connect ORDER-ITEMs to PRODUCT-SPECIFICATIONs and to PRODUCT-PRICES.

Hierarchical data loading is the same as network loading except the step for network connections is impossible, as networks are not supported by the hierarchical data model.

Dynamic Data Loading. Loading a dynamic DBMS database is very simple. The records from each type are gathered together and then loaded into the appropriate record types. Loading is a quick and easy process, almost the inverse of the static database loading process. If the records are supposed to be related to other records in a different record type, then the data loading program must check--on its own--to determine that matching values exist.

Data Update

Data update is the process of modifying the database with new records, deleting existing records, changing relationships (static only) that exist between records, and updating elements within records. Data element update is generally the same for static and dynamic DBMSs. The record is located, the element retrieved and changed, and the record replaced in the database. Beyond element update, there are two significant differences between the static and dynamic approaches.

The first major difference pertains to relationship maintenance. Interrecord relationship maintenance of a static relationship is very different from maintenance of a dynamic relationship. In a static DBMS, the relationship update process consists of issuing a series of DML commands first to locate the record, then to disconnect it from its relationship, then to find the new and proper position, and finally to insert it into the new relationship. To accomplish this task, host language programs are usually written, because the process of correctly maintaining database relationships is often complex. The complexity of the process is directly related to the number of record types and the number of relationships among the record types.

For example, in Figure 2.3 and referring to the data loading example above, if a CUSTOMER is to be related to a different salesperson due to a change in territory, then the SALESPERSON is located, and its relationship with CUSTOMER is parsed until the proper CUSTOMER is found. It is disconnected from the relationship. Since it has to be assumed that the new SALESPERSON-ID is known, the disconnected

The DBMS Viewpoint

CUSTOMER record is connected to the new salesperson using the verbs cited earlier.

Relationship modification in a dynamic DBMS is simple. The element that represents the relationship is located, and its value changed. That's all.

The second major difference relates to the fundamental orientation of the data update. In a static environment, the whole multiple record type database is subject to an update. Therefore, an update is likely to affect many different record types within the same user update transaction. Database update is therefore likely to be a very significant event, involving thousands of transactions in each batch run. By contrast, in a dynamic environment, the update is typically oriented toward a single record type. It is accessed, locked, the update performed, and the record type unlocked. Then the next update transaction is processed.

Database Maintenance

Database maintenance is the process of removing a database from on-line mass storage to off-line mass storage--for example, tape. This off-line mass storage copy has been traditionally referred to as a backup.

The only real difference between static and dynamic DBMS backup is that in a static environment the backup is often one physical file for the whole database, whereas in a dynamic environment there is likely to be one backup file for each record type. In either case the DBMS should provide all the commands necessary to effect the backups in an efficient and effective manner.

Logical and Physical Relationship

From the user's point of view, the database consists of occurrences of records. The DBMS sees the database from the same point of view, except that the definition of record relates to two different concepts.

The DBMS reads and writes physical records from and to mass storage devices. The user obtains and puts logical records from and to the DBMS.

While a logical record may be coincident with a physical record, normally it is not. In most DBMSs, a physical record may contain multiple logical records, and a logical record may span multiple physical records.

Physical Database

In short, the DBMS reads and writes physical records from all of its storage structure components--that is, from its dictionary, its indexes, its relationships (static only), and its data.

As the user reads and writes logical records, the DBMS, in support of the user's requests, reads and writes whatever physical records from and to whatever storage structure components necessary to support the user's logical record. If a user writes a single logical record to a database, the DBMS may place that logical record in the appropriate buffer and not write it--at that time--to disk because the buffer is not full.

Further, the DBMS (static only), in support of the user's logical record write, may have to create and store in the database multiple physical records in support of the user's logical record's relationships to other records. The DBMS may also have to update the addresses for indexes that are changed, because the user's logical record contains indexed elements and the like. In short, a single user's logical record write might generate no physical record I/O, one physical record I/O, or many physical record I/Os.

Physical Database Summary

The physical database from the DBMS point of view consists of a database's storage structure, access strategy, data loading, data update, and database maintenance. The four storage structure components are: dictionary, indexes, relationships (static only), and data. The interactions of these four components to store and retrieve physical records is the DBMS's access strategy. Data loading is the process of initial data storage. Data update, of course, is the process of changing already stored data. Database maintenance is the process of saving an on-line database onto some off-line media.

For the static DBMS, once the database is created, it is also very much bound together through the relationships that relate records to each other. In contrast, the dynamic database has had its record types loaded with records that are yet to be related during retrieval. Certainly, because so much less work is accomplished during the loading process, the dynamic database load is going to be significantly faster than the static load.

A critical difference between static and dynamic DBMSs is in the area of data update. The dynamic DBMS update is oriented towards the single record type, while the static DBMS can handle complex multi-record type updates through its comprehensive locking schemes.

161

The DBMS Viewpoint

The critical differences between static and dynamic DBMSs is tabulated in Figure 9.11.

9.4 INTERROGATION

A DBMS interrogation language is either a set of data manipulation language (DML) verbs that have been incorporated into another host language, or a DBMS self-contained proprietary language, called a natural language.

	STATIC	DYNAMIC
Storage Structure	Multiple component physical files Few physical files Typically dictionary, indexes, relationships and data	Single component physical files Many physical files Typically dictionary index and data
Access Strategy	Primary key and relationship searching via data record processing	Large number of indexes Dynamic matching/merging of record extracts via field values
Data Loading	Complete logical records Careful planning Exact placement Large volumes All or nothing	Record tape by record tape Load what you have Incremental building
Data Update	Very careful Far reaching effects HLI only Periodic data base reorganization	Casual Add new records, fields, etc. at will Seldom needs reorganization
Base Maintenance	Usually one or a few data bases Global save/restore at high level	Many storage structures Careful planning Many commands at low levels

Figure 9.11   Physical Database:
Static and Dynamic DBMS Comparison

Interrogation

The DML interface to either COBOL or FORTRAN is through a specially built interface constructed by the DBMS vendor. The COBOL or FORTRAN acts as the host for the DBMS verbs that the programmer utilizes. Hence the name, host language interface (HLI). A natural language, on the other hand, is a specially created language tailored specifically to suit the needs of the DBMS and to provide an easy to use way of accessing a database.

Compiler languages like COBOL and FORTRAN normally do not have DBMS verbs built directly into them. ANSI COBOL's X3J4 committee is developing COBOL verbs for database access. However, they did not complete the database part of COBOL for inclusion in the probable '84 COBOL project. The ANSI database committee, X3H2, has developed generic specifications for HLI operations for both the network and relational data models. These may be used by DBMS vendors, in any way they wish to interface their DBMS to COBOL, FORTRAN, or any other computer language such as query-update, report writers, and other natural languages. Any of the HLI methods described below are compatible with the ANSI X3H2 specification.

Host Language Interface

The host language interfaces provided by different DBMS vendors differ in two significant ways. The first is in the language invocation format; the second is in the actual capabilities.

HLI Formats. Three methods are popularly used to interface COBOL or FORTRAN to the database. The first is through the incorporation of a series of data manipulation language (DML) verbs like START DBMS, OPEN <database-name>, FIND <record-type-name>, and the like.

The second method is to incorporate a generalized call facility like CALL DATABASE USING <variable, variable,...>. In this case, each of the variables carries information to the DBMS, such as what operation is desired, the name of the record type accessed, selection criteria, and the like.

The third method is a variant of the second. It also is a CALL mechanism, but it uses specially named calls like CALL GET1REK <variable, variable,...,variable>.

In all three methods, the ultimate result is the same: the database is accessed for a specific purpose. The most comprehensive approach is the first, since host language interface (HLI) mechanisms usually have the most user-oriented facilities.

Examples include automatic error procedure invocation, automatic data type translation, and automatic movement of data from the database to the user work area in the program.

The HLI formats seem to be best developed in the static DBMSs. Among the dynamic DBMSs is Computer Science Corporation's MANAGE, which has a well-developed facility. Most other DBMSs seem to have either the second or the third method of host language interface.

HLI Functions.   The HLI is divided into three distinct interfaces: data, control, and commands.

Data Interface.   The interface between a host language program and a database often requires a specially named data storage area within the program that acts as a staging area for data passage to and from the database. Each DBMS creates this interface area differently, so if there is an intent to create programs that are DBMS-independent, an interface subroutine should be built to hold this data interface. Programs then would call the interface subroutine and GET or PUT data regardless of the DBMS employed.

Control Interface.   In a way analogous to the data interfaces, the program has an area for the passage of messages and status indicators to the DBMS regarding the database. In this area there is an especially large difference between the static and dynamic DBMSs. In a static DBMS, the area embraces the database as a whole, so it contains a large number of indicators to tell which database, area, relationship (set), record type, and record occurrence is currently active. These indicators are called currency indicators or cursors.

Because a static network database can be very complex, these currency indicators or cursors have to be just as complex. As the data model becomes less complex, so also do the currency indicators or cursors.

Command Interface.   The commands included are those specially designed to manipulate the data represented by the DBMS's data model. For example, both static data models would have commands to go between owners and members and among members. The network data model could additionally find multiple owners for a member, perform recursive set operations, and the like, while the hierarchical data model cannot accomplish these operations.

164

Interrogation

The dynamic data models would have commands to relate record types together through common data values. The independent logical file data model additionally would have commands to find dependent segments for complex record types, while the relational data model would only be able to select simple records.

Some DBMSs have only simple commands such as FIND, and GET, whereas others might contain complex commands, like FETCH, that represent the combined functionality of FIND and GET. Notwithstanding these variations, the following functions are normally supported by a host language interface capability:

o   Record selection

o   Record insertion

o   Record modification

o   Record deletion

o   Structure navigation

Static and Dynamic Differences.   The DBMS invocation command is functionally similar in both static and dynamic DBMSs. In a static environment, a database OPEN statement has many options. They deal with logging, locking, shared retrieval and update, and exclusive retrieval and update controls. In a dynamic environment the database OPEN statement usually restricts its effects to a single record type, and when it is opened for update, it may automatically be locked from all other use.

The principal difference between a static and dynamic environment is the method by which structure navigation is accomplished. In the static environment there are specific navigation commands to traverse, an owner to a member, for example. In the dynamic environment the programmer is often required to acquire an owner record through a DML call statement, extract the connecting data value, and then use the value as a secondary key selection criterion in another DML call statement to find the members of the relationship.

Natural Languages

DBMSs generally employ three different generic types of natural languages. The first is a procedure-oriented language (POL), which is often used by ILF DBMSs as an alternative to HLI.

The DBMS Viewpoint

The second natural language is report writer. This seems to be implemented regardless of the static or dynamic nature of the DBMS. The third language is query-update. In the static DBMSs except for SYSTEM 2000, the query-update language serves mainly as a quick report writer against a well-structured database rather than as a heuristic research and reporting mechanism. In a dynamic DBMS, the query-update language serves mainly this latter role.

A very important distinction in the types of natural languages is whether each query command accesses the database directly or whether it accesses a subset of the database. Some DBMSs' query facilities cause the initially selected data to be extracted and placed in a "work file" that is then used for the subsequent queries during that session. Others have each query statement within the query session execute directly against the database. Each alternative has its advantages and disadvantages.

For the subset query type, an advantage is that the entire subset of data is consistent and unchanging during the entire query session. A disadvantage is that if the database is updated subsequent to the extract, then reports will not reflect the most current data.

For the direct query type, the advantages and disadvantages are analogously reversed. As a disadvantage, if there is an element, NBR-EMPLOYEES, for example, that represents the number of employees in a department, and then there is a set of employee records, the NBR-EMPLOYEES element might not be the same as the count of employees in the chain if an add or delete is in progress. An advantage is that if the element was AMOUNT-UNENCUMBERED-DOLLARS, then the most current value must be retrieved directly so that funds will not be over-committed.

It is not important whether one type is superior to the other, but whether the database update subsystem can be established knowing which query type is more appropriate.

Language Execution Alternatives. Natural languages usually have three distinct alternatives for execution. The first, interpretive, determines the purpose of each command as it is encountered and then executes it. While interpretive processing is very expensive when a loop is in progress, it offers the maximum flexibility for generation and modification. For example, an interpretive natural language program can generally be inter-

166

rupted in midexecution to change the value of variables and even change, add, or delete statements.

The second type of execution is direct. That is, the language submitted by its user is data to a program that directly executes the request. This is faster than the first type, but does not offer the same execution time flexibility for changing the intent of the interrogation.

The third kind is the compiler variety. The language is submitted to the language's compiler. Once processed, executable code is generated that can be catalogued and then executed just as a COBOL or FORTRAN program can. This third approach is certainly slower in generation, but it is much faster in execution.

Natural language programs should be capable of being created through an editor and capable of being stored--ideally in the data dictionary--for later use or modification. When a natural language program is invoked, it should execute immediately and provide the required output to the terminal or to some other output device, as stipulated in the natural language program.

Procedure-Oriented Language. Procedure-oriented language (POL) is a general term to represent a set of database access capabilities commonly found in ILF DBMSs. While it certainly would be nice to have the POL as an ANSI standard language, and thus be exactly compatible among ILF systems, the DBMS variations of this language are uniform enough among ILF systems to discuss the language as if it were commonly defined. Among the DBMSs that have well-developed POLs are FOCUS, NOMAD, MODEL-204, MANAGE, and ADABAS.

In general, the POL contains clauses for record selection, sorting, terminal prompting, formatting, and the like. In DBMSs that have this type of language, the HLI is seldom used. That is probably why these DBMSs have underdeveloped HLIs. If static DBMSs had POLs, their capabilities would be similar to those illustrated in Figure 9.9. Dynamic DBMSs do have POLs, and Figure 9.10 illustrates their typical capabilities. Discussed below are the minimum capabilities that should be included in a POL.

Automatic Navigation. The POL should provide for automatic navigation of relationships between record types within the same dynamic database and record types of different dynamic databases; they should fully utilize indexes wherever possible, to enhance access.

The DBMS Viewpoint

Selection Expressions. The POL selection expressions should allow for relational operators such as LT, GT, and GE, for the existence or absence of data, for ranges and value masking, and for as many levels of expression nesting as may be appropriate. The selection expressions should also permit selection by computed elements such as sums, counts, minimum, maximum, or average, and the use of the arithmetic operations of addition, subtraction, multiplication, and division. Finally, the selection expression should allow for IF...THEN...ELSE... logic.

Updating. Full updating capabilities should be present in the POL. Commands should allow for single-value changes, multiple-value changes, record additions, and record deletions.

Report Formatting. The report formatting capability should permit column and row totals, sums, counts, sorting by high to low and reverse, headers and subheaders, footers and subfooters, underlining, column headers, line folding, column spacing, control breaks, page breaks, and centering. The output of elements should allow for editing such as zero suppression, floating dollar signs, and variable date formats. It should further allow for multiple element concatenation, and coded value table look-up and the like.

When operations are performed on multiple dynamic databases, the relational operations of matching and merging should be allowed, as well as navigation between databases.

Storage, Editing, and Reuse. Natural language programs should be capable of being created, stored, and edited by their users. Further, both element value arguments and element name arguments should be possible. The structure of a POL program should permit logic branching, terminal prompting, and looping. It should permit command echos, to keep the user aware of a program's progress.

The POL should permit graphic output as well as tabular output. It should support bar histograms, connected point plots, and scatter diagrams. The user should be able to define labels, scales, headers and footers, and point annotation.

External Interfaces and Command Redefinition. The POL should permit the invocation of user-written programs such as COBOL or FORTRAN. Finally, the POL should permit command redefinition for the establishment of a specific audience-oriented language.

POL Summary. A brief review of the types of capabilities contained in a POL quickly leads to the conclusion that this is a complete programming language that often obviates the need for other types of database access languages. The POL is, however, an analytical language, and as such, may not be the most human-efficient language for database access.

Report Writer. A report writer is usually the first language developed after the HLI by the static DBMS vendor. The capabilities are generally similar for both static and dynamic DBMSs, with the exception of record selection and navigation. Report writers are often used as prototyping mechanisms for HLI programs.

The typical capabilities found in report writers include report titles, column titles, row titles, multiple levels of breaks, the ability to skip lines and pages, page headers and footers, output data editing such as floating dollar signs, selection clauses, page counting, logical and physical dimensions for report pages, left and right justification for alphanumeric data, setting and resetting of program variables, multiple report copies, and the like.

Sometimes, report writing capabilities do not exist in a completely separate language but as an extension of one of the other natural languages. The execution alternatives also vary from interpretive, to direct, to compiler oriented.

The fundamental difference between static and dynamic report writers centers not on capabilities, such as footers, headers, and break totals, but on the fundamental nature of the DBMS in which it is used. In a static DBMS, report writer outputs cannot help but mirror the basic design of the database, while in a dynamic DBMS, relationships can be defined that allow any combination of record types to be reported. Figure 9.12 contains an example of report writer language programs.

Query-Update Languages. A query-update language interrogation program is typically able to be constructed as a single sentence, while the POL and the report writer language interrogation may typically contain from 50 to 150 lines. The query normally consists of three types of clauses: output, sorting, and data selection. The output clause usually contains titles and a list of the data elements to be printed. The sort clause specifies the fields for sorting, the sort order, and whether the sorting is to be high to low or reverse. The selection clauses specify the criteria for record selection which may include BOOLEAN operations, relational operators, and the like. A typical query-update sentence might be:

PRINT <element-name>, <element-name>,...

SORTED BY <element-names>,...

WHERE <element-name> <relational-operator> <value>

<boolean operator>

<element-name > <relational-operator> <value>.....

These systems often offer less formatting capabilities than the report writer. They also offer processing logic less capable than that contained in the POL. Their purpose is not to compete with these languages but to offer the ability to do something simple in a simple way. As a result, query-update languages are very popular with the ad hoc interrogator who may wish to obtain only a simple listing of data from one or more record types.

```
COMPOSE:
FOR REPORT SALES,
PHYSICAL PAGE IS 55 BY 55:
DECLARE SUM1 = RCOUNT OF ORDER-ID:
DECLARE SUM2 = RCOUNT OF CONTRACT-ID:
SELECT RECORD IF ORDER OCCURS:
ORDER BY NAME OF CUSTOMER-ID, CONTRACT-ID, ORDER-ID:
FOR CUSTOMER, SKIP TO NEW PAGE, SKIP 2 LINES,
AT END, PRINT (15)$TOTAL NUMBER OF CONTRACTS$, R(45)SUM2:
FOR CONTRACT, SKIP 2 LINES, COMPUTE SUM2,
(45)$MAXIMUM-COST$,
PRINT (15)$CONTRACT-ID$, (30)$DATE-SIGNED$,
AT END, SKIP 1 LINE, PRINT (15)$TOTAL ORDERS$,R(28)SUM1,
(40)$TOTAL VALUE$,R(55)TOTAL-ORDER-COST.
FOR ORDER, AT END, COMPUTE SUM1
END REPORT:
GENERATE ACTIVITY WHERE CUSTOMER-ID EXISTS:
```

Figure 9.12   SYSTEM 2000 Example of Report Writer Program

The typical capabilities that are present in a query-update language include tabular type reporting with titles, sorting by one or more elements, arithmetic functions such as MIN, MAX,

Interrogation

AVG, results of arithmetic formulas, and selection clauses that include arithmetic, relational, and boolean operations.

Again, the fundamental difference between static and dynamic query-update languages centers not on capabilities but on the fundamental static or dynamic nature of the DBMS. In a static DBMS, these query-update languages produce reports that cannot help but mirror the basic design of the database; in a dynamic DBMS, relationships can be defined that allow any combination of record types to be reported. Figure 9.13 contains examples of query-update programs.

```
LIST/TITLE L(5)CUSTOMER-ID, L(15)CUSTOMER-NAME
L(40)CONTRACT-ID, R(50)TOTAL-ORDER-COST,
ORDER BY CUSTOMER-ID, CONTRACT-ID
     WHERE CONTRACT-ID EXISTS:

ASSIGN SALESPERSON-ID EQ 876-87-4932
     WHERE CONTRACT-ID EQ 76498:

REMOVE CONTRACT WHERE CONTRACT-ID EQ 76498:
```

Figure 9.13 SYSTEM 2000 Examples of Query-Update
Language Programs

System Control Capabilities. Specific details about system control capabilities are treated below. The capabilities that are normally available through interrogation language programs include the following:

- o   Audit trails for all updates

- o   DBMS message processing

- o   Backup and recovery

- o   Concurrent operations

- o   Multiple database processing

- o   Security and privacy

The DBMS Viewpoint

Audit Trails. The audit trails for a static DBMS are normally well-developed and centralized to contain a single trail for all updates to the entire database. The dynamic DBMS audit trails are usually not so well developed, and often there is one trail for each dynamic database. This is further reason to keep updating strictly isolated to a single record type when using a dynamic DBMS. Audit trails are normally automatically available, not optional. They are initiated and controlled by a centralized DBA group.

Message Processing. A good interrogation language provides routines for automatic message processing. These enable the language programmer to collect all messages that are to be treated alike into one error-processing routine. The DBMS then transfers to the routine when any of the messages are returned to the program by the DBMS.

Backup and Recovery. In either the static or the dynamic database environments, well-designed backup and recovery is necessary. The DBMS should have the capability to instigate backups from within programs or through POL commands and the ability to automatically start recovery in the event of a database crash. A very important capability for both environments is transaction backout. It enables users to make an update, test the effect of it, and then back it out upon command. See, for example, Figure 6.10.

Concurrent Operations. A static database environment should have well-developed capabilities for concurrent operations. Multiple users should be able to update the database and the same record concurrently, and the DBMS should protect against all cases of execution deadlock. In a dynamic database environment, absolute access is usually granted to one user at a time for each record type.

Multiple Database Processing. Because a static database is potentially very large, complex, and comprehensive, there is little need for multiple database processing. But when there is a need, the host language often provides the only method to accomplish it.

The need for multiple database processing usually arises when the corporate headquarters needs a report that combines sales and marketing data from multiple divisions implementing that have implemented the same type of database.

Interrogation

Ironically, the relationships that exist between multiple static databases are dynamic. The dashed lines in Figure 2.4 illustrate the fact that almost all hierarchical data model databases ultimately need to accomplish multiple database processing.

In the dynamic database environment, multiple database processing is its normal mode in either the host language or the POL. Figure 2.6 depicts dynamic relationships, and Figure 9.10 illustrates how they are parsed.

Security and Privacy. The subschema, when it is carefully constructed, restricts access to specific record types and specific data elements within the records. Beyond that, the DBMS may abort run-units for illegal use of a DBMS operation or the attempted attachment of a record type or element. A run-unit seldom has the ability to manipulate security. Normally, the reverse is true.

Choosing the Right Interrogation Language. Generally, the choice of an interrogation language should follow these steps:

1. Attempt to develop the report/query with the least amount of programming effort possible. That means using either the query-update language, report writer, or POL. What is being developed is a prototype of the task rather than a production report.

2. Demonstrate the result to the person who requested the report/query to determine whether it satisfies the needs. Then change it until it does.

3. When the report or query is acceptable, determine the frequency of operations and estimate the amount of data to be processed, the expected amount of processing time, and the amount of required system control support. Then choose a final programming language for the interrogation that satisfies the combined requirements--assuming that is possible.

4. Leave the prototype report or query in place for use by the requestor--if its performance is tolerable--until its replacement can be created.

173

The DBMS Viewpoint

The following benefits are derived from this process:

o   The prototype is created with minimal human resources.

o   The design is refined with minimal resources.

o   The final product is created only after the design has been validated.

Interrogation Summary

No DBMS can report something it cannot model. This simply means that comparing the overall reporting capabilities of a static DBMS interrogation language to those contained in a dynamic DBMS in order to determine which DBMS is better is like comparing the turning radius of a sports car to that of a bus in order to determine which vehicle is better. The bus cannot have a turning radius of a sports car, because its function is to carry a large number of people, and the design and construction needed eliminates the possibility of a small turning radius. Likewise, the sports car cannot be criticized, as its function is certainly not to transport 30 to 50 persons.

In short, neither the turning radius of the vehicle nor the capabilities of a DBMS's interrogation language alone is sufficient to determine which vehicle or DBMS is better.

The languages available in a particular DBMS probably mirror those functions the DBMS performs in an acceptable manner. No vendor is going to issue a language that will break the back of the system. Finally, the fundamental difference between static and dynamic interrogation languages centers not on capabilities, but on fundamental DBMS design. In a static DBMS, these languages must mirror the basic design of the database. In a dynamic DBMS, these languages allow relationships to be defined to allow any combination of record types to be utilized in the interrogation.

A well-engineered DBMS contains multiple database interface languages. Although there is a growing tendency to rely on natural languages, the compiler interface languages such as COBOL and FORTRAN are important for data loading and data update, for the more complex multiple database processing, and for building DBMS-independent applications.

The point of having multiple languages is to be able to choose the most appropriate language for the job. If a DBMS has only an HLI or a POL, then its vendor cannot be too interested in providing a helpful environment to its users.

A final aspect of interrogation is that it can also be utilized to interface multiple DBMSs for the purposes of accessing static and dynamic databases and transferring data from one DBMS's database to another.

Figure 9.14 compares and contrasts the different types of interrogation languages available from static and dynamic DBMSs.

LANGUAGE	STATIC	DYNAMIC
Host Language	Well-developed, good function and facilities	Poor to acceptable development
Procedure-Oriented Language	None at all	Well-developed, good function and facilities
Query/Update Languages	Underdeveloped Usually no update Constrained by database structure	If developed, then done well
Report Writers	Used only as a shortcut to HLI Constrained by database structure	If developed, usually an extension of POL or QUL.
Application Interfaces	Generally not done except as data dictionaries	Normally done on T/S based dynamic systems

Figure 9.14   Interrogation Languages:
Static and Dynamic DBMS Comparison

9.5   SYSTEM CONTROL

System control principally provides for the protection of the database and for smooth operation of the DBMS. Included in these protections are the following:

- o   Audit trails

- o   Message processing

- o   Backup and recovery

- o   Reorganization

The DBMS Viewpoint

o Concurrent operations

o Multiple database processing

o Security and privacy

o DBMS installation and maintenance

o Application optimization

The principal difference between static and dynamic system control relates mainly to the definition of the word "database." Generally, the domain of each system control capability is the database. In a dynamic DBMS, the database is normally a record type, while in a static DBMS the database is a large collection of interrelated record types. What this usually implies for a dynamic DBMS is that audit trails, reorganization, and concurrent operations are isolated in their effect to the record type. For a static DBMS, these same system control facilities affect the large, complex database as a whole. This means that with a dynamic DBMS, normally just a record type is locked during reorganization. With a static DBMS, normally the whole database is locked during is reorganization. In short, the difference relates to both scope and size.

Audit Trails

Audit trails are logs of database updates. They are supposed to be used for determining the source of an update, rather than fixing a damaged database. The audit trail capability should be able to operate effectively from different run units and in different modes, such as batch, interactive, and exclusive or shared use of one or more databases.

The audit trail should contain enough information to identify correctly the source of the update. Typically, each audit trail transaction should contain at least time and date stamps, database identification, user-identification, and the update transaction itself. An audit trail should additionally be capable of isolating a single user's transactions from within a multi-user environment.

Finally, the audit trail should be capable of being used in conjunction with a previous version of a database to follow the data value changes for the purpose of isolating either an incorrect data value that was added to the database, or to identify the source of a valid but inappropriate value.

System Control

Message Processing

All DBMSs issue messages. So do the application software, the operating system, and many other kinds of system software. A well-organized DBMS has all its messages categorized and summarized in a language that is easy to read and understand. Further, the DBMS should allow the DBA to define additional meanings for each message and to cause the DBMS to automatically catalog all occurrences of certain message types.

Backup and Recovery

The DBMS should contain capabilities to recover databases that become damaged due to software and hardware failures. The facility should be sufficient to prevent the loss of any accepted update.

Backup and recovery should further have the capability to invoke transaction rollback to purge an unwanted update. This rollback capability should be available from either the host or natural language environment.

There are four different classes of backup and recovery. The first two require a backup of the database as the starting point for database recovery. A backup is a complete copy of the database saved onto an off-line media. While the last two types of recovery do not require a backup, sometimes the damage to a database is so extensive that only a database recovery of the first two types is possible. In short, a periodic backup is almost always needed to insure long term safety.

In the first type of database recovery, rerun, the damaged database is dropped and the update job is run again against the backup to generate an updated database.

The second type, roll-forward, means that the damaged database is dropped, a copy of the backup is brought on-line, and the after-images of updated physical records from successful updates are applied to the database to restore it to the point of the crash.

The third type, roll-backward, means that before-images of updated physical records for all updates from the most recent update to the most recent quiet point are applied to the database, so that its status is rolled back in time to the quiet point, at which time the update jobs are restarted.

The fourth type of recovery combines the third and then the second, in succession. The effect is that the database is rolled back to a quiet point, and then successful transactions subsequent to the quiet point are applied up to the last successful transaction.

The difference between static and dynamic DBMSs, with respect to backup and recovery, relates to the definition of databases. In a decentralized, that is dynamic, environment, backup and recovery of the individual record type is certainly faster. Integrated, multiple-record type dynamic databases are more difficult to accomplish, specifically because of the decentralized logical and physical structures.

Reorganization

There are two types of reorganization, logical and physical. Logical reorganization refers to processes the DBMS makes available to change the database's logical structure.

Logical Database Reorganization. As database applications evolve, there will be a need to add new information types (element, record, or relationship) to the database, to modify existing types, and to delete unnecessary types. The process of accomplishing these changes is called logical reorganization. Logical database reorganization should include the capability to add new element types and new record types, and to change element characteristics and interrecord relationships.

Physical Database Reorganization. Physical reorganization refers to the processes the DBMS makes available to bring the physical order of the database back into close relationship to its implied logical order. Generally, when a database is initially loaded, its physical order closely matches its logical order. As record instances are deleted or added, the DBMS automatically rearranges the physical order of the database.

Physical database reorganization is needed because the physical organization of the database becomes inefficient with respect to updates and interrogations. Simply, this means that programs are now operating more slowly than when the database was "new." Normally this is because the storage structure has become fractured. Physical database reorganization, then, is the process of recapturing the efficiency that was in the "new" database.

Physical database reorganization capabilities should include the ability to add or delete indexes, reload data records to optimize data placement, and to increase index performance.

System Control

Static and Dynamic Differences. The difference between static and dynamic DBMSs is striking. Logical reorganization in a dynamic DBMS is easier and is accomplished more rapidly because the domain of the dynamic record type is very restricted. Some dynamic DBMSs even allow changes to the individual record type without physical reorganizations. The static DBMS, however requires physical reorganization for all but the simplest logical database changes.

As might be expected, the domain of the affected record types in a static DBMS is much larger than in a dynamic DBMS. Consequently, physical database reorganization in a static DBMS is more extensive and consumes greater resources.

Concurrent Operations

The term "concurrent operations" embraces two very different concepts: mixed data interrogation or update operations to the same database, and database operations such as physical reorganization and database loading. Generally, the latter types of database operations require exclusive control of the entire database for a static DBMS, or of a single record type for a dynamic DBMS.

For mixed data interrogations or update operations to the same database, the following DBMS types need to be identified:

o   A single database DBMS is one that permits commands to access only the single database that is then under its control.

o   A multiple database DBMS is one that permits commands to access different databases that are under the control of the single instance of the DBMS.

o   A multi-user DBMS is one that can process commands from multiple run units.

o   A single-threaded DBMS is a multi-user DBMS that can execute only one command at a time and cannot service another command until the processing is finished for the first command.

o   A multi-threaded DBMS is a multi-user DBMS that can concurrently execute the multiple commands from the multiple run-units against a database.

179

The DBMS Viewpoint

o   A multiple database processing DBMS is one that
    can concurrently access multiple databases dur-
    ing a single executing instance of a run-unit.

o   A single-threaded, multiple-database DBMS is
    one that can execute only one command at a
    time while serving multiple users against multi-
    ple databases.

o   A multi-threaded, multiple database DBMS is one
    that can concurrently execute multiple com-
    mands from multiple run-units against multiple
    databases.

Ideally, every DBMS should be both multi-threaded and multiple
databased. That, however, may not be needed for certain
applications. Further, such an environment requires a large
machine. Typically, such environments require three million bytes
of memory for the DBMS, its buffers, the teleprocessing monitor,
and the like.

In general, the dynamic DBMS can perform the multi-
threaded, multiple database set of operations with less DBMS
vendor software than is required with a static DBMS. This is
because in the dynamic database, the record types are typically
physically independent, and other aspects of their storage structure are also very physically and logically decentralized.

It is not safe to run certain operations along with others--
physical database reorganization and data updates, for example.
The DBMS should automatically preclude some commands from
operation while others are in execution. A well-designed DBMS
handles the occurrence of execution deadlock. It discovers that
it has happened and takes the necessary steps to terminate it.

The DBMS should also contain sophisticated locking mechanisms for use at both the database and the record type levels, as
needed by the application.

Multiple Database Processing

Multiple database processing is the ability to access data from
different databases from within the same HLI or natural language run-unit. Most dynamic DBMSs have very well-developed
multiple database processing capabilities. This is because they
require multiple database processing to accomplish any significant database applications. The dynamic DBMSs allow this multiple database processing in a variety of interrogation languages.

System Control

In a static database however, the database is naturally more complex, so these DBMSs usually provide this capability only through the host language interface--COBOL.

Security and Privacy

Database use necessitates sophisticated security and privacy, since well organized collections of corporate data can be readily available through easy-to-use, rapid-access natural languages. To protect the database, security and privacy facilities must be carefully examined. Some DBMSs allow concentric rings of ever-increasing control. Others have access keys on specific elements, records, and operations. Finally, some DBMSs allow definition of access profiles. Each profile should be able to specify the records that are allowed to be accessed, the data elements within the records, the operations allowed on the data, and the privacy that can be imposed on data selection, retrieval, and modification. Security and privacy should be easy to define and modify but impossible to break.

Enforcement of security and privacy is accomplished in a variety of ways. Some facilities are under DBMS control; others are integrated into the operating system. While the latter is more secure, it almost certainly implies that the DBMS must be an integral component of the hardware vendor's system software.

DBMS Installation and Maintenance

The DBMS vendor should provide well-developed procedures for the DBMS's installation. A full range of tests to verify the DBMS's correct operation should be included. The DBMS vendor should include a sophisticated test database so that errors in the installation, or subsequently found bugs, can be duplicated on the test database and then reported to the vendor. To help isolate DBMS bugs, the DBMS vendor should provide well-defined procedures that users can employ to determine whether the problem is with the user's program or the DBMS.

The DBMS vendor should provide well-defined procedures for creating special versions of the DBMS that increase certain types of DBMS efficiencies. For example, dramatic changes in application performances can be achieved by manipulating the number of buffer pools and their sizes, DBMS subroutine overlay configurations, placement of storage structure components on different computer channels and drives, and so on. It should be stated however, that in a diverse application environment, DBMS changes that dramatically benefit one application often cause another to degrade by an equal amount.

The DBMS vendor should also provide procedures to enable the DBA to limit the kind of functional modules available to the user. For example, if the modules that permit security and privacy changes are deleted from the run-time copy of the DBMS, it becomes quite difficult to change these access controls.

Finally, the DBMS should have a well-documented mechanism for incorporating new versions of the DBMS and for transferring a database of the DBMS's old storage structure format to a new one.

Application Optimization

The DBMS should have sophisticated tools for discovering which areas of a database application are performing slowly. The DBMS vendor should provide well-documented methods for performance-testing new and improved versions of host or natural language program design, database design, storage structure construction, buffer allocation, and storage structure and DBMS work file placement.

Finally, the DBMS vendor should provide sophisticated performance-monitoring tools to analyze ongoing database system performance and to determine the rate of database deterioration so that the required reorganization can be performed.

System Control Static and Dynamic Differences

The main difference between static and dynamic DBMSs in the area of system control (see Figure 9.15) relates to the fundamental definition of the word database. In a dynamic DBMS, the word database usually means record type, while in a static environment, the word database means many interrelated record types.

Since most system control operations affect a single database, a dynamic logical record type reorganization is possible without physically affecting other record types. In a static database environment, a logical record type reorganization is likely to require the entire database operation to stop and not continue until the reorganization is completed.

In short, the principal difference between static and dynamic system control is in the span of control of the various system control operations. The functions most affected by the difference are audit trails, backup and recovery, reorganization, and multiple database processing.

	DBMS TYPE	
SYSTEM CONTROL FUNCTIONS	STATIC	DYNAMIC
AUDIT TRAILS	Acceptable for complex data-bases sometimes content definable	Acceptable for simple data-bases but generally not able to track multi-record type structures
BACKUP AND RECOVERY	Acceptable for complex data-bases and on-line environ-ments of multiple databases	Acceptable for simple data-bases and on-line environ-ments of multiple record types. Difficult to track up-dates to multiple record types through recovery.
MESSAGE PROCESSING	Acceptable, but normally no message database, nor content definable	Same as static
REORGANI-ZATION	Often requires complete data-base reload for even small logical change.	Effects of logical change able to be restricted to single record type, thus reloading effect is restricted.
SECURITY & PRIVACY	Generally not O/S linked, and is restriced to specific func-tion denial versus user access profiles	Same as static
MULTIPLE DATABASE PROCESSING	Limited as static DBMS normally supports single complete database	Excellent facilities as capa-bility is prerequisite to normal processing.
CONCURRENT OPERATIONS	Good multi-user, multi-thread, and locking. Some DBMS operations require database lock	Good multi-user for different record types. Often locks at record type level for update. Some DBMS operations re-quire exclusive DBMS use if storage structure is centralized
APPLICATION OPTIMIZATION	Good facilities as DBMS offers many ways to restruc-ture DBMS configuration, and database structures	Features available to optimize performance are limited as DBMS only supports simple environment
INSTALLATION AND MAINTENANCE	Few cross-checking facilities facilities to validate correct DBMS functions	Same as static

Figure 9.15 System Control: Static and Dynamic DBMS Comparison

For example, if there was an operating system failure during the time an on-line, multi-user update DBMS environment was operating, a database recovery event would recover all databases that are active under a particular copy multi-user DBMS. In a static environment, all the record types in all the active databases would be recovered.

In a dynamic environment, the recovery might neither be as effective nor as complete as the static environment. For example, suppose all record types were backed up over a weekend, and updates occurred on Monday and Tuesday to some dynamic record types. On Wednesday, these updated record types (databases) were removed from the on-line environment. The failure then happens on Thursday. If the removed record types are not on-line, then the Monday-on recovery cannot occur against those off-line record types. In such a case, the DBMS should notify the DBA that record types are missing from the on-line environment, and that until they are brought on-line, the recovery cannot be completed.

System Control Summary

Even though the areas of system control have been presented separately, they almost always interact. For example, suppose that application optimization indicates that the application is slowing. In response, physical database reorganization is invoked to bring the database back into optimum condition. To accomplish database reorganization, the concurrent operations capability of EXCLUSIVE USE must be invoked. If the security and privacy facility permits user profiles with specification of database operational verbs, then only the DBA should be allowed to activate the REORGANIZE verb.

9.6 DATABASE MANAGEMENT SYSTEM SUMMARY

A database management system contains four very tightly interwoven components. The logical database is the mechanism for understanding the functional area database that is to be handled by this computer software. The physical database represents the storage layout of the loaded data, the loading subsystem, the update subsystem, and the mechanism for database backup. The interrogation component, through its series of languages, enables users to access the database in an efficient manner. Finally, system control enables the whole database environment to be maintained in a safe manner.

9.7 DO YOU HAVE THE RIGHT DBMS?

To serve an application effectively, a DBMS should have these two characteristics:

o The DBMS should not get in the way of accomplishing the application.

o The DBMS should help make the application simpler to design, implement, and maintain.

If you are bending, contorting, blazing new trails, then you very likely have the wrong DBMS. If you discover yourself doing these things, STOP!

Reexamine the process by which you chose the DBMS. Maybe you don't have a database application, or perhaps you are attempting a dynamic application with a static DBMS, believing that by using a static DBMS you can force order and control. Or conversely, maybe you are using a dynamic DBMS for a static job, with the result that the lights dim every time a large complex report is run. Figure 9.16 sets forth the results of choosing the right or wrong DBMS for a particular application.

APPLICATION	DBMS	
	DYNAMIC	STATIC
DYNAMIC	OK	Never ending Endless reorganization Often aborted projects
STATIC	Slowed performance Lessened integrity Very high CPU/IO Too expensive to maintain	OK

Figure 9.16 Application and DBMS Cross-Matrix

Remember, it is far wiser--and easier--to make a quick turn shortly after starting than it is to persevere to the end. Often, the only thing waiting for you at the end if you begin with an inappropriate decision is a complete and total failure. To recover from that, you will probably have to convince somebody that this is a glorious opportunity to burn several metric tons of data, programs, and money, and then start all over.

The process of developing a prototype is very useful in determining which DBMS is right for your application. Not long after the first prototype demonstration, it will be clear that either the changes will never stop, or that they have settled down. In the former case, a dynamic DBMS is the only choice; in the latter, a static DBMS is preferable.

If you know your application, and if you are thoroughly familiar with the major DBMSs, choosing the most appropriate DBMS is not at all difficult.

9.8   REVIEW QUESTIONS

1.   What is the single most important difference between static and dynamic databases? How is this manifest in DBMSs?

2.   Describe the components of a data definition language.

3.   In the context of a DBMS, what is the difference between a logical database record and a physical database record?

4.   What are the advantages and disadvantages of static relationships compared to dynamic relationships?

5.   What is the role of a subschema?   Define its construct.

6.   Define access strategy, and compare static access strategies with dynamic access strategies.

7.   Contrast the processes required for static and dynamic data loading.

8.   List and compare the different types of interrogation languages.   What are the likely static and dynamic differences?

9.   List and describe the components of system control. What are the likely static and dynamic differences?

10. Which type of DBMS is suitable for a "low-budget," simple application? Why?

11. Is is true that a dynamic DBMS requires less application work? Explain.

10 Controlling Database Risk

10.1 RISK FACTORS

One thing should be very clear by now: the database approach is not a computer science--it is a management science! It just so happens that the computer is a good vehicle for implementing database projects, and that instead of expending hundreds of person-years on specialized software development, organizations can make use of a generalized solution, the DBMS, in conducting a broad range of information management activities.

Not only are database projects a big effort, they are also performed at a considerable risk. This risk can be both managed and minimized, however. The overview of database project methodology presented in Chapters 5 through 8 describe practical ways to significantly reduce waste or redundancy in the use of project manpower. Selecting the right staff, getting them trained, and using the right DBMS is also critical. Six additional factors bear heavily on the accomplishment of the elusive goal, success:

o Application risk

o Management assistance

o Documentation

o Consistency

o   Definable policy

o   Policy coherence

10.2   APPLICATION CHARACTERISTICS

Knowing when not to do something is important--especially in database applications. Not all applications are ready for the database approach. To attempt an implementation prematurely will very likely result in failure. There are four characteristics that can be measured to help calculate application risk: relative value, complexity, technical competence, and starting conditions.

Relative Value

Just how important are the data represented by the databases? If they are lost, will the corporation fail? Will significant sums of money be lost if the database is fatally damaged? For example, the loss of a brokerage house's customer database could certainly lead to its failure. The point of this characteristic is that if the data are critical, then the amount of attention paid to the database must also be critical.

The key indicators of high relative value are inordinate pressure to be on time, the level of management served by the data, and the perceived value of the data as measured against corporate existence. If all these items are always communicated in high-pitched voices, then you have a very high-risk application in terms of relative value.

Complexity

Database applications tend to be very complex, because the database approach offers to integrate and manage many peoples' data in one automated repository and to keep all the data straight. Further, database offers to enable all those people to access and update the data without killing each other. Moreover, all this is supposed to be done very fast.

Some typical measures of complexity are the number of users served; the number of operational modes, that is, batch or interactive; the number of record types within each database; the approximate data volume; the distribution of the numbers of programs in the various interrogation languages; the requirements for critical system control features such as audit trails, backup and recovery, and security; and the number of different databases that have to be coordinated for single functions. Whenever a database application is obviously complex, the risk of undertaking it is high.

Technical Competence

The skills required by the database participants are quite var ed, ranging from being very functionally knowledgeable to being fully technically capable.

The knowledge required by the functional users is in the area of conceptual design. The less knowledgeable these people are about the real import of the database, the higher the risk that a good database design cannot be built. Two types of functional knowledge must be present. The first can be acquired from academic training; the second comes only from long-term organizational tenure.

The DBMS specialist, the interrogation specialist, and the system control specialist have to be very skilled in both DBMS and data processing. Again, if these persons have to learn their skills in addition to performing them, the risk of application failure is again high.

The other database staffer, the database specialist, is required to possess both DBMS and functional skills. This is because the primary role of the database area specialist is as mediator-translator between the functional area personnel and the technical personnel.

Once more, if all these staff do not possess a good leve' of experience with database, then their chances of successfull accomplishing a complex, high-value database project are quitɛ low.

Starting Conditions

A simple way of determining starting conditions is to look at the existing situation. If the whole organization is not well organized or well managed, and if confusion rules policy, work flow, conflicting goals, and the like, then the organization, while it may desperately need a database, is nowhere near ready for one. It must put its house in order before it can automate its information systems. Automating a fundamentally disorganized business will only serve to demonstrate its disorganization.

One measure of starting conditions is the trouble the organization may have had with previous standard access applications. If it cannot get a simple one right, there is no hope for a database application. Again, the bigger the mess, the higher the risk.

Application Risk Summary

Determining whether it is safe to undertake a particular database application is not simple. It must nevertheless be done. Since implementing database applications is neither simple nor cheap, one of the alternatives must be "no implementation." The decision not to implement a particular application in database does not have to be permanent; the conditions that make it inappropriate at a given time may change. The functional users may someday decide to come together on policies, and sufficient training may someday have been acquired by the database staff.

10.3 MANAGEMENT ASSISTANCE

Management must remember that a database is in essence a treaty that binds all of its users. An organization must be ready for database before it can be successfully implemented.

As stated in Chapter 1, if database is understood to be only a technology, it can still be implemented at any time. But if it is only a technology, its success can be characterized only by such technological feats as loading 5 billion characters, running 17 transactions per wall clock second, having 7 levels of hierarchy without any redundancy, or having one record type or data element represent 8 different purposes. Never kid yourself into thinking that you have a real database if those are your primary measures of success.

Database success is characterized by organizational quality, coherent policy, efficient decision making, and multipurpose high-integrity data, as well as the multitude of ways in which functional users can collect present data, compare them to the past, and project future corporate strategies.

The role management must play, is first to understand what a database really is, and second, to understand that if the organization is not correctly postured, database should not be tried. The exercise of creating the conceptual specification produces a valuable result in its own right: it is a statement of just what part of database is actually possible. The real commitment to database, that is, the really significant expenditure of money and time, does not come until the implementation phase.

Even if a database application is not implemented immediately, or ever, the conceptual specification reveals the depth and the breadth of agreement in corporate traditions and organization, as seen through the harsh realities of operational policies. A concrete expression of that kind of reality is rare--and of incalculable value.

The two ways in which management can really help are to support the establishment of realistic schedules and to provide the long-term commitment needed to bring about some measure of success. It must be remembered that the development of the database project's conceptual specification is the codification of good management practice, and that could well take several iterations to accomplish, with one or two unexpected discoveries along the way.

Good Scheduling

One of management's basic tasks is to create schedules. Confronted with an an activity that is purely technical, a schedule for the achievement of concrete objectives can readily be made. But since database is not purely technical, its schedules must be established as objectives rather than as absolute deadlines.

The conceptual specification is best done in four to eight months. Its objectives are clear, and its scope is to determine the feasibility of a database project, not to implement it, even though part of the conceptual specification is a prototype. Once a determination is made concerning database practicality, the schedule for the second phase, implementation, can be estimated with some degree of accuracy.

The only part of the implementation phase that is unpredictable is obtaining quality data for database loading. Since old data were probably not collected using any really coherent set of policies, putting old data into good shape can be very time-consuming or even impossible. It is therefore conceivable that all the database project software could be ready long before the data are ready to load.

Long-Term Commitment

One of the main reasons often given for implementing database is the desire to upgrade organizational quality with respect to organizational efficiency, effectiveness, and accuracy. The commitment management must make, therefore, is to continue the development of ways to enhance the organization through the use of computerized data that model the behaviors necessary for successful operational, tactical, and strategic planning.

Controlling Database Risk

Data Architecture Plan

There are many ways to look at an organization. The traditional way is through the processes performed within discrete functional areas, such as finance, planning, marketing, facilities management, personnel, and the like. Such a view is typically set forth in information system studies that follow the IBM Business Systems Plan (BSP) methodology. The BSP conclusions often call for the specification and implementation of traditional systems like accounts payable/receivable (AP/AR) for finance; product tracking, pricing, and sales reporting for marketing; and payroll and staffing for personnel. In addition to an information systems plan, the BSP often calls for the development of an information architecture. However, it is to be defined in terms of the proposed or analyzed information systems that have been identified as needed in the study. Typically, there is a one-to-one relationship between an information system and its data.

Clearly, while the information systems identified in a BSP are all-important and ultimately must be implemented, it does not follow that there should be a one-to-one relationship between an information system and its data. If there were, then for every 100 information systems there would be 100 databases, and it would be very unlikely that there would be interdatabase data consistency such that the databases could "talk" to each other.

If the organization is to attempt a database system, then, in addition to identifying the all-important information systems, there must also be developed an integrated database design, which must exist prior to the development of the BSP-recommended information systems. That is, there must first be a data architecture to serve as the foundation, upon which these all-important information systems will be built. If there is such a data architecture foundation, many benefits will follow. For example, there could be nonredundant systems to collect data and feed the integrated databases, quite apart from the often redundant reporting systems. Redundant data collection--one for each information system--is probably the single most significant reason why there are masses of data everywhere but information nowhere.

A data architecture is an information organization that reflects the data interaction of the fundamental business functions of the enterprise. Upon this information architecture foundation, information systems, which are implementations of specific sets of business functions, can be built easily and simply. For example, with the data architecture for a company in place (see Figure 10.1), the critical processes that use the data, such as sales and demand reporting, can be established as a discrete application, with the certain knowledge that all the data used by this application come from a centralized marketing information database that also might contain corporate customer and prospect data, and that these data are available to corporate planners as they predict requirements for research and manufacturing. Data interaction is possible only because the data were initially defined within a completely integrated whole.

Since the information systems called for in the BSP are certainly processes, the data flow diagram is an excellent device to represent them graphically. Its ability to represent nested hierarchies of processes allows complex collections of interrelated activities to be easily visualized. Once these DFDs have been defined down to the lowest level, the development of clearly specified information system modules is rather straightforward.

To represent a data architecture, the most appropriate tool is the entity-relationship (E-R) diagram. The E-R diagram presented in Figure 6.3 shows the interaction of entities through generalized relationships. As the database specification proceeds, these generalized entities and relationships become record types, data integrity rules, and data transformation rules. The methodology involves the iterative refining and binding of a generalized graphic description to human and computer procedures and programs.

If the E-R diagramming technique is used to create the organization's data architecture graphic, then the product of this effort will certainly be too large and too complex to comprehend easily. For example, if an E-R diagram for a moderate-size marketing control data-based system is about 75 entities, then a combined E-R diagram for 20 such databases within a single organization might be over 1000 entities.

To help distinguish the forest from the trees, entities on the data architecture E-R diagram should be abstracted to as many more generalized diagrams as are necessary to represent the data architecture simply. An example of an abstracted E-R diagram is provided in Figure 10.1. The term "abstracted" is employed rather than "higher-level" to indicate that the E-R diagrams need not be wholly contained sets or subsets of each other, as is required in data flow diagrams.

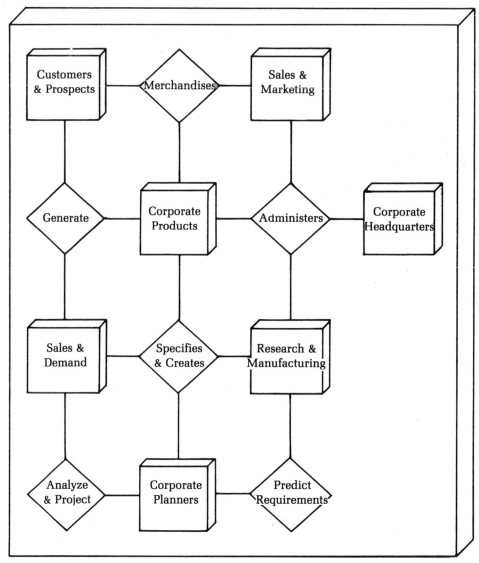

Figure 10.1   Data Architecture Entity-Relationship Diagram

For example, the entity CUSTOMER appears both in Figures 6.3 and 10.1. Although that is certainly acceptable in a set of E-R diagrams, it would not be allowed in a collection of leveled DFD diagrams. The reason for this diminished rigor in the E-R approach is that the E-R diagram is not intended to provide a specification, as is the DFD diagram, but a direction.

Taken together, these E-R diagrams represent the data architecture of the organization. At the highest level of abstraction, the major interactions are very general, and on the more detailed diagrams, the interaction of entities are more specific.

A senior-level staff member should analyze the set of organizational E-R diagrams and determine the most appropriate sequence and strategy for implementing each logical collection of entities as a separate database project, ever mindful of the need for data integration. The extent to which data integration is possible depends on many factors, such as the types and kinds of computers, the DBMSs employed, and the physical grouping of participating organizations.

Once database applications are identified and their implementation sequence determined, the project methodology can be used to implement them. To successfully accomplish the projects, database administration must be properly activated to provide the proper DBMS environment and to assist in the definition of the interface points to other projects. Once these activities are underway, the data architecture plan is certainly set in motion, and then the development of BSP-recommended information systems can proceed quickly.

Management Assistance Summary

The main reason management should provide support for the development of a database is that the database is really management's system. Most other data-processing systems have been for others in the organization. For example, accounting and finance is for the accountants; all the statistical and mathematical packages are for the scientists and engineers; and inventory, manufacturing control, and distribution are for the logistics personnel.

A database system is for management. It gives management the controls it needs to assess the present, look into the past, and project the future--and that is what management is all about.

10.4 DOCUMENTATION

Documentation has always been the last thing done in a standard access system. It cannot be that way in a database system. Documentation must be the first thing done. That is because the orientation of a database is not toward the design and implementation of large collections of interlocking programs and files, but toward the definition and establishment of coherent collections of data that are accessed and manipulated by canned software.

The documentation required for a database must be created during each of the three database project phases. At the end of the first two phases, conceptual specification and implementation, the documentation serves two purposes. First, it is a testimony to what has just occurred; second, it is a proposal for the next phase.

The documentation that results from the third phase must contain completely updated versions from the prior two phases, because it is also necessary to fully comprehend the entire project. A database project's documentation must also include all the DBMS reference manuals, training manuals, and other documentation. Counting all these additional books, the documentation of a complete database system might well approach fifty binders. That's a stack about 75 percent taller than Wilt Chamberlain.

To hold, maintain, control, update, and access all this material in any efficient manner requires that a majority of it be stored as data elements and records in the metabase.

If the metabase contains all the documentation, then any portion of it can be changed and regenerated--on demand. Surprisingly, the number of characters taken up by about 12 feet of normal-size documentation is only between 100 and 200 million characters. That is only one-fifth the size of a moderately large database. And since all of it has to be created in typewritten media at some time anyway, why not make it useful as well? In this case word processing would not be the appropriate technology for collecting and storing the data, because word processing would not put the data into the elements and record formats that are prerequisite for data access and update.

Another reason for putting documentation in a metabase is that it can then be made part of the normal work process of systems analysis and programming. Instead of recording material on paper and then transforming it into electronic media, it can be recorded directly onto the metabase with the full support and assistance of the metabase's editing and validation. Traditional paper copies could be produced as reports from the metabase.

Using this system, the status of a database project could be computed more easily and accurately. The metabase analysis programs could compare the current progress with that of prior projects and make predictions about completion time.

The point is that 9 out of every 10 data processing people consider traditional documentation to be a colossal waste of time, effort, and energy, because everybody wants to work on the present and the future, not the past, and the past is exactly what documentation is all about. And they are absolutely right! Because of this, documentation is seldom accomplished in any timely or accurate manner. Traditional systems have survived in spite of this lack of high-quality documentation simply because documentation was not on the project's critical path. Not so for database applications. A database cannot be successful without proper, correct, and efficient documentation. Because database documentation is on the critical path of the database project, the nature of documentation must change; that is, it must become both timely and accurate. The metabase accomplishes this transformation because metabase documentation

- o Becomes part of the work process;

- o Is captured in an easier and more efficient manner;

- o Greatly reduces the unnecessary redundancy;

- o Is stored as elements and records, thus making it accessable, and capable of being modified;

- o Is always available in the most current form.

10.5 CONSISTENCY

Consistency, as defined by the American Heritage Dictionary (1978), is "(1) Agreement or logical coherence among things or parts. (2) Compatibility or agreement among successive acts, ideas, or events." This seems to be another definition created especially for database. In short, consistency permits and promotes accountability.

If there is not a careful plan for consistency, the only thing database will have accomplished--looking back ten years from now--will be to have replaced the file (a simple-technology data store) with a database (a complex-technology data store), and the program with the nonprocedural language program. There will still be the same lack of conformity and relatability; only this time, the lack of conformity and relatability will be more rampant in the organization, be more damaging to the organization's ability to correctly forecast changes, and be more difficult to correct.

Consistency applies to almost every aspect of database. It must be present during the conceptual specification phase while policy is built, while the prototype is built, and finally, it must be considered when the initial selection of the DBMS is made.

In the implementation phase, consistency must apply to the incorporation of policy into each of the data update programs or in the automatic DBMS procedures. It must be especially prominent in all the system control components, so that the database is well protected and preserved.

Finally, in the production and administration phase, consistency must be the keystone of the metabase. It permits the efficient search for and identification of just the modules that have to be changed. In short, consistency is essential for effective database usage.

10.6 DEFINABLE POLICY

A policy is a precise statement of what goes on in an organization. Fuzzy policies are the source of many arguments. Clearly the implementation of that sex code policy in Figure 1.1 was not thought through. No one really knew who was what, when, why, or under what conditions, long after the change was implemented.

In the database approach, there must be policies for everything. They must exist for all record types, all data elements, all data integrity rules, and all data transformations. These rules must be defined publicly, reviewed publicly, and approved publicly.

Defining policy is a management issue, because if management does not initiate consistent policies, maybe the programmers will have to, or the ad hoc users, or the data input clerks. To be sure, all policy decisions will be made. The only question is whether they will be made according to a universally applied corporate policy. If no formal policy has been created and turned into automatically executing computer code, then there will never be any long-lasting database integrity.

10.7 POLICY COHERENCE

Policy coherence is the effective articulation and coordination of management decisions within an organization. There must be policy agreement within a community of database users about the boundaries that demark different policy areas. Determining these limits is critically important, as they are the maximum boundaries of the database. For example, if agreement is not possible on the data values for the sex element, then it must not be included in the database, because different users are sure to update and retrieve personnel on the basis of these unreliable element values.

Getting agreement on the data values to represent the two sexes should be simple. Accomplishing agreement on larger issues can be quite difficult. For example, are proposed but not yet signed contracts to be included in the database? What about contracts that have been terminated or fulfilled? What about permanent employees, temporary employees, prospective employees, retired employees? What about personnel assignment to projects? Or the allocation of management costs to projects? Or the computation of direct and indirect overhead, commissions, computer time chargebacks, and the like? What about historical data? Do you keep it forever, a year, five quarters, or what? All of these issues must be decided and agreed to by all parties before the database specification leaves the conceptual specification phase. Simply stated, no element should ever be included in a database until there is ironclad agreement on each and every one of its characteristics.

10.8 RISK CONTROL SUMMARY

Since each of the six factors described in this chapter can significantly influence a database project, it is important that each factor be evaluated as accurately as possible and that steps be taken to minimize its potential negative impact. For some of the factors, minimization of negative impact involves upgrading technical competence, improving starting conditions, reducing complexity, and the like. Other factors--management assistance, for example--involve understanding the need to establish realistic project schedules, realizing that undertaking a database project is a long-term decision, and establishing a good solid data architecture plan.

Regarding the data architecture plan, some projects can begin without such a plan as long as the design of the database is engineered naturally and is modelled to contain obvious integration interfaces to connect it with other implemented systems. However, development of the data architecture plan should not be postponed indefinitely. Selection of an appropriate DBMS critically affects the integration capability of any set of database projects. The DBMS should have a rich data structure for modelling data, good separation between logical database definition and physical database implementation, well-developed natural languages so as to avoid host language interface programming, and good control mechanisms for protecting and updating the database system.

If all six of these risk factors are not addressed and resolved before a database is attempted, then the organization is simply courting self-destruction.

10.9 REVIEW QUESTIONS

1. List and explain the four application characteristics that contribute to the measurement of application risk.

2. The term relative value has a specific meaning in this chapter. What is relative value? What are the key indicators that measure it?

3. In the context of application risk, what are the measures of complexity?

4. Discuss the similarities and differences between being very functionally knowledgeable and being completely technically capable. Which applies to logical database design, and which to physical database design? Why?

5. Give an example, using the criteria presented in Chapter 10, of a company that you feel is not ready to implement a database.

6. What role should management play in implementing and maintaining a database system?

Review Questions

7. Why should old data be considered suspect prior to performing an initial database load?

8. Why is documentation the first thing to be done in developing a database project, whereas in the traditional data processing environment it is usually the last thing to be done?

9. Briefly describe the documentation needed in each of the three database project phases.

10. What are the advantages of having a metabase as compared with traditional modes of documentation?

11. Corporate policy plays an important role in a database project. What areas within a database project must be governed by policies?

12. Explain why a database project is more a management challenge than a technical challenge.

13. Rank the six risk factors according to your view of their importance. Give the reasons for your ranking.

14. Why are well-defined policy and policy coherence so important to the success of a database project?

15. How do the data integrity model and the data transformation model relate to definable policy and policy coherence?

11 Summary

11.1 THE DATABASE MATRIX

The successful implementation of a database system requires careful attention to its four aspects: technology, staff, the project, and DBMS. In each of these four areas, the same four topics were addressed: logical, physical, interrogation, and system control, so that a cross-reference of information can be achieved. Figure 1.5 illustrates the interaction of these areas and topics.

11.2 TECHNOLOGICAL CONCEPTS AND DBMS

The technology surrounding the database approach has evolved out of necessity. In the 1950s, data processing personnel started to build solutions to problems, one at a time. Soon there were many different solutions. And then someone wanted to solve a problem that required data from two different previously solved problems, and then three, and so on. Finally, the interrelationship of all these solutions got so large and so heavy that it crumbled and crushed all beneath it.

Out of the ruins database was born--twice. Its first entrance was as a complete programmer replacement system. These systems were called self-contained language systems. Database's second entrance was as a way to insulate the large COBOL systems from the effects of small changes. These systems were called host language interface (HLI) systems.

205

Summary

Shortly after these systems started to flourish (about 1968), someone would not buy one because it did not have some of the capabilities of the other. For example, there was a need to use a natural language to access the host language database, and there was also a need to use COBOL to access the self-contained database. At that moment the golden rule of business took over, and the vendors of each type saw the merits of the other. The business golden rule is this: "The one who possesses the gold has the rule."

The technical capabilities of the various DBMSs have continued to be improved since then. The first area of evolution was to expand the capabilities of data models. That has settled down to four: network, hierarchical, independent logical file, and relational. And since ANSI has standards development only in the network and relational data models, the number is likely to shrink to these two. Next, there was evolution in the development of supports, such as advanced interrogation languages. Today these new and improved languages greatly ease the development and maintenance of database projects. System control capabilities, such as audit trails, reorganization, concurrent operations and the like, have also received generous attention. A more recent push is in the area of data dictionaries (or metabases).

There is still a healthy competition among the various systems representing the technologies. Only recently have some of the vendors started to understand the value in having both static and dynamic relationships--at the same time--in their DBMSs. For example, IBM's SQL/DS can exist alongside IMS, FOCUS can report from IDMS, and Cullinet (formerly Cullinane) has demonstrated an integrated relational-like reporting from IDMS's static network database, and also automatic downloading of IDMS database data to personal computers.

11.3 STAFF DEVELOPMENT

Training is best accomplished when there is a problem to resolve. At that point relevance is never questioned. Training programs must contain intriguing workshops that enhance the learning of DBMS and database concepts and facilities. With workshops, two problems must be avoided. First, if the workshop is too closely related to real work problems, then too much time may be spent on performing the activities in the workshop rather than on learning the DBMS material. Second, if the work-

206

shop material is too foreign, then again too much time will have to be spent learning the activities in the workshop before any of the DBMS or database material is learned. The workshop therefore must provide discussion and also allow for concentration on the material.

Subsequent to development of staff, small database projects have to be undertaken so that the material learned in class can be tested in nonsuicidal situations.

11.4 THE DATABASE PROJECT

The database project is unique in that it can actually be fully operational before much work or money is expended. This is possible through prototyping. Prototyping generally requires a dynamic DBMS with good natural languages. The only static DBMS that can create prototypes is SYSTEM 2000. That is because, of all the static DBMSs, only SYSTEM 2000 was initially developed as a self-contained language DBMS.

The first phase, conceptual specification, could be considered a reality assessment. Its product is the determination of what is both practically and politically possible. The results of the conceptual specification phase must be publicly reviewed and revised until a consensus is reached.

The second phase, implementation, involves the greatest amounts of time and money. The logical database's data integrity model developed during the conceptual specification phase is transformed into the DBMS's data model and DDL. The data transformation model is transformed into the various critical subsystems of data loading and data update. Finally, the system control subsystems are created and thoroughly tested. At this point, the database system can be loaded and be declared operational.

In the final phase, production and administration, the database system operates and grows in three ways: data, interrogation, and structure evolution. If properly done, the implementation phase incorporates provisions for change. If a database application cannot grow and evolve without major database and program surgery, then in all probability the wrong DBMS has been chosen. If this is the case, do not continue. Cut your losses and change!

But, given the right environment, project methodology, and tools, the database approach assists in the development of the modern information system in the following ways:

Summary

o An organization-wide data structure can be created to serve multiple applications concurrently.

o New applications can be built without redundant
analysis, design, programming, and data collection.

o The organization is able to create common
definitions of data, which in turn permit more
effective communication of needs, plans, and
policy among the participating organizational
units.

o Data can be directly accessed by a wider audi-
ence without the traditionally required skills or
training.

o Data processing resources are able to be more
efficiently utilized because natural language
data access requires less analysis, design, documentation, and maintenance.

11.5 MANAGEMENT'S ROLE

The role of management in a database project must be perva-
sive. Management must be heavily involved in the conceptual
specification phase. No decision in this phase should be made
without a full presentation to management about the database's
corporate implications. As the database project progresses to
implementation, the active role of management diminishes.
Management is called into action only when a policy has to be
changed for some technical reason.

The next and major role of management is that of a database system user. All the natural languages are management's to
use. Management should directly connect itself to the database
and use its power to get just the right information needed for
sophisticated decision making.

11.6 SUMMARY AND CONCLUSIONS

As I stated at the outset, in the preface, the database approach
has been developed to the point that the complicated technology
on which it is based does not show any longer--or shouldn't. As
a result, database's real face, that of a management challenge,
cannot be avoided.

DBMSs whose technology are as difficult to scale as Mt. Everest is to climb are increasingly being discarded into the same junk heap that already contains the bones of other technical diotheres.

Careful planning is critical. Do not move too fast. Do use prototypes. Do recognize that static and dynamic DBMSs are different and that you cannot use one for the other's applications. Finally, remember that since database can only mirror organizational quality, it cannot be used to effect an organizational cure.

Techniques that enable organizations to operate efficiently must already have been implemented before a database project is attempted. If a corporation is not efficiently organized, database is simply not possible. To have database is to be organized.

11.7 REVIEW QUESTIONS

1. Why is a database system oriented more toward management than towards technicians?

2. What will happen to a database project if its cornerstone is the DBMS rather than the combination of the data integrity model and the data transformation model?

3. What are the characteristics of a contributory DBMS? What are the characteristics of a DBMS that impede project progress?

4. What are the characteristics of projects that benefit from a static DBMS? From a dynamic DBMS?

5. Describe the conditions that would indicate that the wrong DBMS has been chosen for a project.

6. Describe the symptoms of a poorly defined set of policies. Outline a plan to remedy the situation.

7. What is meant by the statement, "To have database is to be organized?"

Appendix I
Comparison of DBMS Characteristics

Interrecord Relationship Mechanism and Data Model			
STATIC		DYNAMIC	
Network	Hier-archical	Indepen-dent log-ical file	Relational
Total IDMS/R	IMS SYSTEM 2000	ADABAS FOCUS	IDMS/R

Note : CULLINET Software has released its newest DBMS version, IDMS/R, which enables both traditional network and relational data structures to be built in the same database. The relational data access languages interact with the relational tables, with the traditional network structures, and with combinations of the network structures and relational tables.

DBMS   LOGICAL DATABASE

IDMS/R--static

- o CODASYL-like network with multiple set types.

- o Good check and procedure clauses.

- o Good selection of data types.

- o Multiple databases through major and minor schemata.

TOTAL

- o Very restrictive two-level network.

- o No check and procedure clauses.

- o Restricted data types.

- o Multiple databases only by recompiling and reloading/creating intersection records.

Appendix I

DBMS	LOGICAL DATABASE

IMS

- o Multilevel hierarchies.
- o Logical structure binds physical placement.
- o Only basic data types.
- o Multiple databases through IMS controlled twin concepts.

SYSTEM 2000

- o Multilevel hierarchies.
- o Separation of logical structure and physical placement.
- o Good selection of data types.
- o Check and procedure clauses through user exits.
- o Multiple databases through HLI commands.

Appendix I

SYSTEM   LOGICAL DATA BASE

ADABAS

     o   Record type (ADA file) is two-level
         structure.

     o   Good selection of data types.

     o   Almost no automatic integrity checks.

     o   Multiple ADA-file processing through
         natural language and host language
         interfaces.

FOCUS

     o   Record type is multilevel hierarchy;
         should be restricted to two levels.

     o   Very good selection of data types plus
         automatic editing and integrity checks.

     o   Multiple databases through relational
         operators.

IDMS/R-dynamic

     o   Flat relational tables with logical keys.

     o   Automatic table creation through menu-oriented DDL

     o   Referential integrity between tables

     o   Traditional pointers built between tables at
         user option to increase relational performance.

     o   All IDMS/R data types.

     o   Multiple databases through relational operators.

SYSTEM   PHYSICAL DATA BASE

IDMS/R--static

- o Allocation of physical files through DMCL, a physical file allocation language.
- o Area concept with record type allocable to multiple physical files.
- o Primary key and set selection for record access and navigation.
- o Secondary key access to record type.
- o Complex data loading, very time consuming.
- o Field update easy. Relationship updates modify pointers in-place rather than through record delete and re-add.
- o Superior backup and restore capabilities.

TOTAL

- o One storage structure for each record type.
- o Primary key and "set" access to member.
- o Complex data loading necessary to compensate for restricted logical database structures.
- o Field update easy; relationship update difficult.
- o Adequate backup and restore capabilities.

Appendix I

SYSTEM	PHYSICAL DATA BASE

IMS

- o Single organized storage structure.

- o Close binding between logical and physical structures.

- o Primary key access through multiple access methods; automatic database navigation via logical twins.

- o Moderately complex data loading.

- o Field update easy; relationship update only through deletes and re-adds.

- o Acceptable backup and restore capabilities through IBM utilities.

SYSTEM 2000

- o One or more hierarchies per storage structure.

- o Logical and physical orders different.

- o Primary key is user-enforced.

- o Secondary key at any level points to relationships for SYSTEM 2000 controlled navigation before records are selected.

- o Data loading simple to complex, depending upon level of reporting or updating efficiency desired.

- o Field update easy; global updates for indexed fields. Relationships update through deletes and re-adds.

- o Acceptable backup and restore capabilities.

Appendix I

SYSTEM	PHYSICAL DATA BASE

ADABAS

- o One storage structure divided into three physical files for all ADA-files.
- o Primary key is user-enforced.
- o Secondary keys point to data record.
- o Very simple ADA-file at a time loading.
- o Field and relationship updating very simple.
- o Very good backup and restore capabilities.

FOCUS

- o Records of the same type are stored on pages that are interlinked with one or more physical files.
- o Primary and secondary key access.
- o Simple data loading.
- o Field and relationship update very simple.
- o Acceptable backup and restore capabilities.

IDMS/R--dynamic

- o Tables allocated dynamically and automatically.
- o Primary and secondary key access.
- o Easy data loading through automatic screens or reformated source data files.
- o Field and relationship updating simple.
- o Superior backup and restore capabilities.

Appendix I

SYSTEM · INTERROGATION

IDMS/R--static

- o Well-developed HLI that can access both relational and network structures.

- o Logical view facility enables structures to be perceived as flat tables.

- o All other languages are constrained to report according to logical database structure dictates that are embedded in storage structure.

TOTAL

- o Acceptable HLI.

- o All other languages are constrained to report according to logical database structure dictates that are embedded in storage structure.

IMS

- o Acceptable HLI, has automatic multihierarchy access.

- o No other languages.

SYSTEM 2000

- o Very well developed HLI with multiple database access verbs.

- o Automatic structure navigation and record sorting.

- o Query language is rich and efficient because of sophisticated storage structure and access strategy.

SYSTEM   INTERROGATION

ADABAS

- o Acceptable to good HLI with record sorting.

- o Query language adequate.

- o New POL is acceptable.

FOCUS

- o HLI minimum capabilities.

- o POL very sophisticated; replaces most programs.

IDMS/R--dynamic

- o HLI is same as IDMS/R above.

- o Rich relational query language with menu or command modes.

- o Access to network structures and relational tables.

SYSTEM   SYSTEM CONTROL

IDMS/R--static

- o Audit trails can be content-defined.

- o Backup and recovery is superior.

- o Reorganization costly, but required only if serious database design error has been made.

TOTAL

- o Audit trails can be content-defined.

- o Backup and recovery is adequate.

- o Reorganization (through reload) required more often than IDMS/R, since small application changes often require database design changes.

IMS

- o Audit trail design for database recovery.

- o Backup and recovery well developed.

- o Reorganization very costly, but can be controlled through decentralized storage structures.

SYSTEM 2000

- o Audit trails cannot be content-defined, since they are for recovery only.

- o Backup and recovery acceptable.

- o Reorganization is sophisticated for both physical and logical database design changes.

SYSTEM   SYSTEM CONTROL

ADABAS

      o   Audit trails cannot be content-defined, since they are for recovery only.

      o   Excellent backup and recovery of one whole database.

      o   Excellent reorganization.

FOCUS

      o   Audit trails cannot be content-defined, since they are for recovery only.

      o   Backup and recovery is acceptable.

      o   Reorganization is excellent.

IDMS/R--dynamic

      o   Audit trails content-defined,

      o   Superior backup and recovery.

      o   Reorganization is excellent.

Appendix II
Related Readings

Atre, Shaku. Data Base Management Systems for the Eighties. Wellesley, Mass.: QED Information Sciences, 1983.

------. Data Base: Structured Techniques. John Wiley, New York: 1980.

Auerbauch Publishers, Practical Data Base Design. Reston, VA.: Reston Publishing Company, 1981.

Bassler, Richard A., and Logan, Jimmie J. The Technology of DBMS's. Alexandria, VA.: College Readings, 1976.

Bender, Paul S. Resource Management., New York: John Wiley, 1983.

Bernstein, Philip A., ed. ACM SIGMOD (May 30-June 1). New York Conference Committee: The Association for Computing Machinery, 1979.

Berstein, Rothnie, and Shipman. Distributed Data Base Management. New York: The Institute of Electrical and Electronics Engineers, 1978.

Biggs, Birks, and Atkins. Managing the Systems Development Process. Touche Ross Management Series.: Englewood Cliffs, N.J.:Prentice Hall, 1980.

Borkin, Sheldon. Data Models: A Semantic Approach for Data Base. Cambridge, Mass.: MIT Press, 1980.

Bowman, Sally. Graphical Data Management in a Time-Shared Environment.. Santa Monica, Calif.: System Development Corporation, 1968.

Cagan, Carl. Data Management Systems. Los Angeles, Calif.: Melville Publishing Company, 1973.

Appendix II

Canning, Richard. The Debate on Data Base Management. Vista Calif.: EDP Analyzer, Canning Publications, 1972.

Carabillo, Virginia, ed. SDC Magazine. Volume 9, | 11. Santa Monica, Calif.: System Development Corp., 1968.

Chen, Peter. Data Base Management, Monograph Series NO. 6. Wellesley, Mass.: Q.E.D Information Sciences, 1977.

Chen, Peter. Entity Relationships. In Proceedings of the Second International Conference on Entity-Relationship Approach. Sangus, Calif.: The ER Institute, 1981.

CODASYL Systems Committee, Selection and Acquisition of DBMS's. CODASYL Systems Committee and Sponsoring Organizations. New York, N.Y.: 1975.

CODASYL Systems Committee, Featured Analysis of DBMS's. CODASYL Systems Committee. New York, N.Y.: , 1971.

Computer Sciences Corporation, Introduction to MANAGE Data-Base Inquiry. Los Angeles, Calif.: Computer Sciences Corporation, 1980.

Conference Committe. Third International Conference on Very Large Data Bases. Very Large Data Bases (October 6-8). Tokyo, Japan, 1977.

Cullinet Corporation. IDMS Documentation. Westwood, Mass.: Cullinet Database Systems, 1981.

Curtice, Robert and Jones, Paul. Logical Data Base Design. New York: Van Nostrand Reinhold Company, 1982.

Date C. J. An Introduction to Database Systems. Volumes 1,2. Reading, Mass.: Addison-Wesley Publishing Company, 1983.

Davis, B. Data Base Management Systems User Experience in the U.S.A. Manchester, England. National Computing Conference Centre Limited Publications, 1975.

Davis, Gordon B. Management Information Systems. McGraw Hill Series in Management Information Systems. New York, N.Y.: McGraw-Hill, 1974.

Appendix II

Dean, A.L. <u>Data Description, Access and Control</u>. 1971 ACM SIGFIDET Workshop. San Diego, Calif.: November 11-12, 1971.

----------. <u>Data Description, Access and Control</u>. 1972 ACM SIGFIDET Workshop. Denver, Col.: November, 1972.

DeMarco, Tom. <u>Structured Analysis and System Specification</u>. New York: Yourdon Press, 1978.

----------. <u>Controlling Software Projects</u>. New York: Yourdon Press, 1982.

Epstein, Robert. <u>A Tutorial on INGRESS</u>. Berkeley: Electronics Research Laboratory. College of Engineering. Univ. of Calif., 1977.

Everest, Gordon C. <u>Database Administrator: Organization Role</u>. Univ. of Minnesota: Management Information Systems Research Center. Graduate School of Business. 1973.

----------. <u>A Taxonomy for Understanding Data Structures</u>. Univ. of Minn.: Management Information Systems Research Center, 1979.

----------. <u>Characteristics of Inter-Entity Relationships</u>. Univ. of Minn.: Management Information Systems Research Center, 1977.

Flavin, Matt. <u>Fundamental Concepts of Information Modeling</u>. New York: Yourdon Press, 1981.

Fodor, John. <u>Reference Manual for DBS/IRX</u>. Dayton, Ohio: Intra Corporation (NCR), 1982.

Fossum, Barbara. <u>Data Base Associated Activities with CODASYL</u>. San Antonio: Sperry Univac, 1975.

Fry, Teorey. <u>Design of Database Structures</u>. Englewood Cliffs, N.J.: Prentice-Hall, 1982.

Gane, Chris and Sarson, Trish. <u>Structured Systems Analysis: Tools and Techniques</u>. Englewood Cliffs, N.J.: Prentice-Hall, 1979.

Appendix II

Gold, Mark E. Uses of Natural Languages., Palo Alto Calif.: Institute for Mathematical Studies in the Social Sciences. Stanford Univ., 1966.

Gruber, Synnott. Information Resource Management. New York: John Wiley, 1981.

Honeywell Information Systems. IDS/II & DM-4 Reference Manual. Phoenix: Honeywell Information Systems, 1978.

Horowitz, Ellis and Sahni, Sarlaj. Fundamentals of Data Structures. Woodland Hills, Calif.: Computer Science Press, 1976.

Hubbard George U. Computer Assisted Data Base Design. New York: Van Nostrand Reinhold Company, 1976.

Hutt, A.T.F. A Relational Data Base Management System. New York: John Wiley, 1979.

Infodata Systems. INQUIRE (DBMS Documentation). Rochester, N.Y.: Infodata Systems, 1980.

Inmon, William H. Effective Data Base Design. Prentice-Hall Series in Data Processing Management. Englewood Cliffs, N.J.: Prentice-Hall, 1981.

Intel Corporation. SYSTEM 2000 (DBMS Documentation). Austin, Texas: Intel Corporation, 1980.

Kapp, Leben. IMS Programming Techniques. New York: Van Nostrand Reinhold Company, 1978.

Katzan, Harry Jr. Computer Data Management and Database Technology. New York: Van Nostrand Reinhold Company, 1975.

King, W. F. ed. ACM SIGMOD (May14-16, 1975). San Jose, California: International Conference on Management on Data, 1975.

King, Judy M. Evaluating Database Management Systems. New York: Van Nostrand Reinhold Company, 1981.

Appendix II

Kroenke, David. Database Processing. Chicago: Science Research Associates, 1978.

---------. Database: A Professional's Primer. Chicago: Science Research Associates, 1978.

Lohman, Severance. Differential Files: Their Application. David W. Taylor Naval Ship Research and Development Center under contract N00014-75-C-1119.

Lowenthal, Eugene, ed. ACM SIGMOD (May 31-June 1). New York: Conference Committee, The Association for Computing Machinery, 1978.

Lyon, John K. The Database Administrator. New York: Wiley-Interscience Publication, 1976.

Martin, James. An End-Users Guide to Data Base. Englewood Cliffs, N.J.: Prentice-Hall, 1981.

---------.Principles of Data Base Management. Englewood Cliffs, N.J. Prentice-Hall, 1976.

Martin, James and McClure, Carma. Software Maintenance: The Problem and Its Solutions. Englewood Cliffs, N.J.: Prentice-Hall, 1983.

Mathmatica Corporation. RAMIS II Reference Manual. Mathmatica Products Group, Princeton Station Office Park, Princeton, New Jersey, 1977.

McElreath, Jack T. IMS Design and Implementation Techniques. Wellesley, Mass.: QED Information Sciences, 1979.

Meadow, Charles T. Applied Data Management. New York: John Wiley, 1976.

Members of Database Admininistration Project. The Database Administrator. GUIDE Executive Board. Information Systems Division. Information Management Group. 1972.

Myers, Glenford J. Composite Structured Design. New York: Van Nostrand Reinhold Company, 1978.

Appendix II

National CSS Corporation. <u>NOMAD2</u> (<u>DBMS Reference Manual</u>). Wilton, Conn.: National CSS, 1981.

Olle, T. William. <u>The CODASYL Approach to Data Base Management</u>. New York: John Wiley, 1978.

Orr, Kenneth T. <u>Structured Systems Development</u>. New York: Yourdon Press, 1977.

Page-Jones, Meilir. <u>The Practical Guide to Structured Systems</u>. New York: Yourdon Press, 1980.

Palmer, Ian. <u>Data Base Systems: A Practical Reference</u>. Wellesley, Mass.: QED Information Sciences and Ian R. Palmer, 1975.

Perkinson, Richard C. <u>Data Analysis: The Key to Data Base Design</u>. Wellesley, Mass.: QED Information Sciences, 1984.

Perron, Robert. <u>Design Guide for CODASYL DBMS's</u>. Wellesley, Mass.: QED Information Sciences, 1981.

Perry, William E. <u>Data Base Management NO. 10</u>. Wellesley Mass.: Q.E.D. Information Sciences and William E. Perry, 1980.

---------. <u>Evaluating the Costs/Benefits of DB</u>. Wellesley Mass.: Q.E.D. Information Sciences and William E. Perry, 1982.

---------. <u>Managing Systems Maintenance</u>. Wellesley, Mass.: QED Information Sciences, 1981.

Peters, Lawrence J. <u>Software Design: Methods and Techniques</u>. New York: Yourdon Press, 1981.

Ross, Ronald G. <u>Data Base Systems Design, Implementation and Maintenance</u>, New York: AMACOM, 1978.

Rothnie, James B. <u>International Conference on Management of Data</u>. New York: Association for Computing Machinery, 1976.

Rustin, Randall, ed. <u>Workshop on Data Description Access</u>. ACM SIGMOD Workshop, May 1 - 3, 1974. Association of Computing Machinery, New York, 1974.

----------. Workshop on Data Description. ACM SIGMOD Workshop on Data Description, Access and Control, Ann Arbor, Michigan, May 1-3 1974, 1974.

Semprevivo, Philip C. Teams in Information Systems Development. New York: Yourdon, 1974.

Software AG of North America. ADABAS Reference Manuals. Reston, Va: Software AG of North America, Inc., 1979.

Sperry Information Systems (UNIVAC). DBMS-1100 (Reference Manual). Minneapolis, Minn.: Sperry Univac Corporation, 1981.

Sprowls, Clay. Management Data Bases. Santa Barbara, Calif.: Wiley/Hamilton, 1976.

Sundgren, Bo. Theory of Data Bases. New York: Petrocelli Charter, 1975.

Ullman, Jeffrey. Database Systems. Potomac, Md.: Computer Science Press, 1980.

----------. Principles of Database Systems. Potomac, Md.: Computer Science Press, 1982.

U. S. Air Force, Office of Areospace Research. Survey of Automated Language Processing. Bobrow, Fraser, and Quillian. Cambridge, Mass.: Air Force Cambridge Research Laboratories. 1966.

U.S. Department of Commerce. National Bureau of Standards. Institute for Applied Technology. A Computer System for Inference Execution, by R. E. Levien. Washington, D.C.: Government Printing Office, 1966.

U.S. Department of Commerce, National Bureau of Standards, Institute for Applied Technology. Design of Reliability by J. Sable. Government Printing Office. Washington, D.C.: 1965.

U.S. Department of Commerce, National Bureau of Standards. CODASYL Data Description Language. by Fredrick Dent. National Bureau of Standards Handbook 113. Government Printing Office, 1974.

Appendix II

U.S. Department of Commerce. National Bureau of Standards. Institute for Computer Sciences and Technology. Moore, Kuhns, and Trefftzs. Computer Science and Technology. Government Printing Office. Washington D.C.: 1977.

U.S. Department of Commerce. National Bureau of Standards. Institute for Applied Technology. Final Report: Joint AFLC/ESD/MITRE Advanced Data Management (ADAM) Experiment, (AD-648-226). by B.F Char, et al. Defense Documentation Center (NTIS), Washington D.C.: 1967.

U.S. Department of Commerce. National Bureau of Standards. Institute for Applied Technology. On-Line Translation of Natural Language, (AD-654-595). by Charles H. Kellogg. Defense Documentation Center (NTIS), Washington D.C.: 1967.

U.S. Department of Commerce. National Bureau of Standards. Institute for Applied Technology. Proceedings of the 2nd Symposium of Computer Centered Data Base Systems, (AD-625-417). by C. Baum, et al. Defense Documentation Center (NTIS), Washington D.C., 1965.

U. S. Department of Commerce. Center for Programming Science and Technology, Modeling and Measurement Techniques for Evaluation of Design Alternatives in the Implementation of Database Management Software. by D.R. Deutsch. Washington, D.C.: Government Printing Office, 1979.

U.S. Department of Commerce. National Bureau of Standards. Institute for Applied Technology. Second Congress on the Information System Sciences. by James M. Burrows, et al. Defense Documentation Center (NTIS), Washington D.C., 1966.

Vorhaus, Alfred H. The Time-Shared Data Management System. Santa Monica, Calif.: System Development Corporation, 1967.

Wegner, Peter. Programming with ADA. Englewood Cliffs, N.J. Prentice-Hall, 1980.

Weinburg, Victor. Structured Analysis. New York: Yourdon Press, 1979.

Appendix II

Wiederhold, Gio. <u>Data Base Design</u>. New York: McGraw-Hill, 1977.

Yoa, S. Bing. ed. <u>Very Large Data Bases</u>. West Berlin, Germany: Association for Computing Machinery, New York, N. Y. September 13-15, 1978.

Yourdon, Edward. <u>Managing the System Life Cycle</u>. Yourdon Press, 1982.

----------. <u>Structured Walkthroughs</u>. New York: Yourdon, 1978.

Index

Index

Index

normalized processing   155

-O-

operations   136
organization's data view   194

-P-

page splitting   152
PERFORMANCE
     statistics   114
     tuning   110
PHYSICAL DATABASE
     physical database   30, 46, 151
     reorganization   35, 105, 114, 178
     specification   84
     transformation   106
     validation   97
PHYSICAL RECORD
     construct   152
     free space   152
POINTERS
     pointers   24
     rings   24
     space   152
policy determination   201
primary key   31, 108, 149, 152
procedure oriented language   167
process oriented interrogation   88
production and administration   123
production and administration consistency   200
program based relationships   24
program based semantics   4
programmer productivity tools   93, 102, 124
PROJECT
     documentation   198
     phase schedules   63
     prototype   59

-Q-

query update language   91, 166

Index

DATE DUE

MAY 2 7 1987	